# ROCK LEAD GUITAR *Solos*

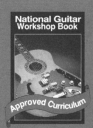

National Guitar Workshop Book — Approved Curriculum

## The Ultimate Guide Playing Great Leads

### GLENN RILEY

Alfred, the leader in educational publishing,
and the National Guitar Workshop,
one of America's finest guitar schools, have joined
forces to bring you the best, most progressive
educational tools possible. We hope you will enjoy
this book and encourage you to look for
other fine products from Alfred and the
National Guitar Workshop.

National Guitar Workshop Book — Approved Curriculum

Alfred

ISBN 0-7390-3159-7 (Book & CD)

This book was acquired, edited and produced
by Workshop Arts, Inc., the publishing arm of
the National Guitar Workshop.
Nathaniel Gunod: acquisitions, managing editor
Matthew Cramer: music typesetter and assistant editor
Timothy Phelps: interior design
CD Recorded at Big Bang Studios, Baltimore, Maryland

Cover photo: Jeff Oshiro

# Table of Contents

A compact disc is included with this book. Using the CD will help make learning more enjoyable and the information more meaningful. The symbol below appears at the top of the first page of every solo. It will help you find the track on the CD.

**With Solo, Track 00**
**Backing Track, Track 01**

The CD provides recordings of the author performing the solos in this book and backing tracks for you to practice with.  Track 1 will help you tune to the CD.

Have fun!

# About the Author

G.I.T. graduate **Glenn Riley** started playing guitar at the age of 12. He resides in Baltimore, Maryland, where he has been teaching guitar since 1991. Glenn is co-author of the National Guitar Workshop/ Alfred's *7-String Guitar* with Tobias Hurwitz, who features Glenn on his instrumental CD, *Painted Sky*. During the summers, Glenn can be found teaching at both the Nashville and Connecticut campuses of the National Guitar Workshop. He also teaches at the Baltimore DayJams campus, for which he authored the rock bass curriculum.

## Acknowledgements

Glenn would like to thank: his lovely wife, Dana, for her patience and support, Nat Gunod, Tobias Hurwitz, Matt Cramer, Ronni Santmyer at Big Bang Studios, Reinhard Schmidt, Jay Turner, Mom, Dad, Granny, Amber Jean, Dave Smolover, Paula Abate, the National Guitar Workshop, DayJams, his family, friends, students, Andy "Sy" Seyler, the Reagan Years ('80s tribute band), Rosso Music Center, Steve Zold and his first guitar teacher, Jody Bender.

# Introduction

Many guitarists wonder how great guitar solos are created. This book will teach you how to turn what may seem to be a barrage of scales into legendary licks. In each chapter, you will find complete solos, each in a specific style, usually that of a specific master. Each solo is accompanied by a step-by-step analysis covering the chord progressions and scales used, thus providing all of the information you need to understand the solo's creation and execution. Use the accompanying CD to hear each solo as it should be played. The CD also features backing tracks for each example, allowing you to improvise your own solos.

Before each solo you will find a box explaining the effects settings used to approximate each artist's signature sound on the CD. For example, here are the effects settings for the solo in the style of Eric Clapton:

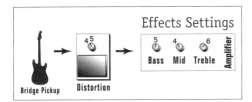

Of course, every effects pedal, amplifier, pickup and guitar has its own, unique sound; the exact same settings on two different sets of gear will sound very different. The settings this book provides will be most useful when combined with the guitar sounds you hear on the CD.

This book assumes that you are familiar with:

- Reading standard music notation and/or tablature
- Scales: major, minor, pentatonic and the modes of the major scale
- Rock techniques such as bending, tapping, sweep picking, arpeggios and so on
- Music theory, including chord construction and diatonic harmony (using Roman numerals to describe chord progressions, such as I–IV–V)

A technique section has been provided on pages 94–95 to serve as a quick reference guide. For a thorough course on music theory, check out the National Guitar Workshop's *Theory for the Contemporary Guitarist*, by Guy Capuzzo (Alfred #16755).

The rock guitar solo was born in the 1950s and evolved primarily from within the 12-bar blues form. In the hands of greats like Chuck Berry and Bill Haley, the guitar was brought to the forefront of the music scene. Their six-string explorations opened the door for a new generation of guitar masters to build upon.

Influenced and inspired by the blues greats, artists such as Jimi Hendrix and Eric Clapton went wild. In creating new sounds, rhythms and textures, these artists gave the guitar a new life—thus paving the road to the future. With the array of effects, technique and styles available today, there is no limit to what you can accomplish with your guitar.

Now, let's play!

# Chapter 1

## The Style of Eric Clapton

Eric Clapton was influenced at an early age by American blues and roots music. His lead style is bursting with soul and blues flavor. Clapton credits players such as Chuck Berry and Bo Diddley as his first major influences. With these influences and his own creative imagination, Clapton creates solos that are nothing less than pure magic. The following example provides a tasteful blues-influenced solo in the style of Eric Clapton.

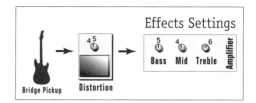

Effects Settings

**With Solo, Track 2**
**Backing Track, Track 3**

*Served via Slow Hand*

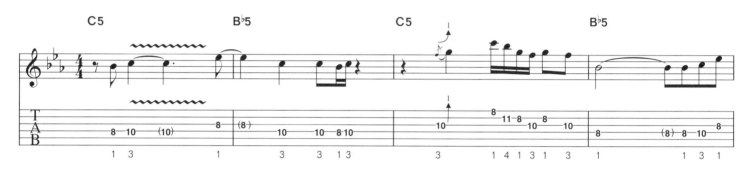

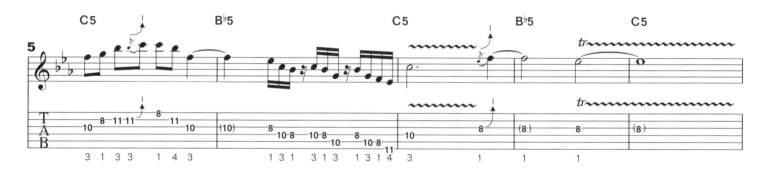

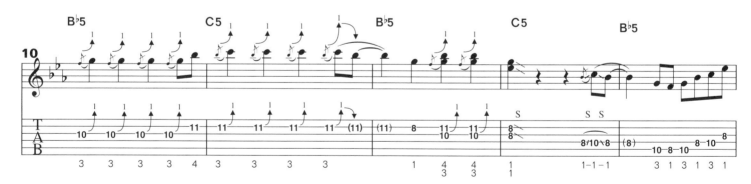

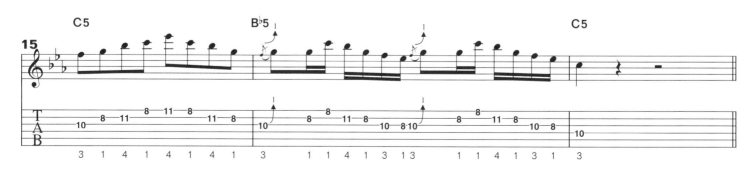

## The Chords and Scales

### The Chords

This very common and simple minor rock i–♭VII chord progression uses basic power chords.

### The Scale

Since power chords contain no 3rd, there are many scale choices from which to choose. Eric Clapton is very fond of both major and minor pentatonic scales. C Minor Pentatonic works beautifully over this C5–B♭5 groove. The example solo is played using only the C Minor Pentatonic scale in 8th *position* (four to six frets starting at the 8th fret).

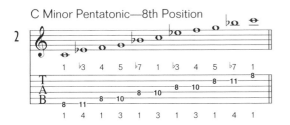

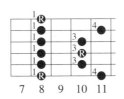

Ⓡ = Root or tonic of the scale.

## Analysis

Clapton breathes life into the notes he plays by using plenty of bends and vibrato, but he rarely uses the pinky of his left hand. Hammer-ons and pull-offs are also big parts of his technique.

One of the most unique things about Clapton's soloing style is his phrasing and delivery. His soloing achieves a melodic, vocal quality by taking breaths (rests) between licks and ideas.

The opening four bars can be viewed as *call and response* (a method of phrasing a lick that resembles a question followed by an answer) using short, tasteful pentatonic licks. Notice that the root note of the B♭ chord is being emphasized in **bar 4**.

**Bar 6** contains a descending lick that is made via a *pattern sequence* (repeating a short idea through a pattern, beginning on a different pattern-note each time).

A nice bending *motif* (a short rhythmic or melodic figure which repeats) appears in **bar 10** and continues on through **bar 11**. Repeating ideas in this manner helps hold the interest of the listener.

The ascending line in **bars 14–16** creates a climactic ending in contrast to most of the previous short melodic phrases. The solo ends on the root of the tonic chord, giving it a sense of completion.

## The Style of Jimmy Page

Jimmy Page began playing guitar at the age of 13 after hearing an Elvis Presley tune. After playing in a band called The Yardbirds with fellow guitar-great Eric Clapton, Page went on to form Led Zeppelin. He incorporated flavors of rock, blues, folk and Indian music, giving his style great diversity. Page is also known to occasionally use a violin bow on his guitar strings. The following solo is in the style of "Stairway to Heaven"—a classic Jimmy Page lead.

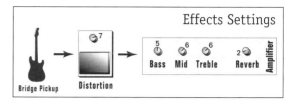

**With Solo, Track 4**
**Backing Track, Track 5**

## Mystery Steps

*8va = Ottava alta.* Play an octave higher than written.

## The Chords and Scales

### The Chords

This tune is in the key of A Minor. The i–♭VII–VI progression is played as a two-measure riff. The Amin and G chords are divided evenly across the first measure, while the F chord takes all of the second.

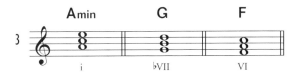

### The Scales

Since the chords set up an A Minor key center, A Minor Pentatonic and A Aeolian are the best scale choices. A Minor Pentatonic works perfectly over the Amin chord. The Aeolian mode adds flavor to the G and F chords.

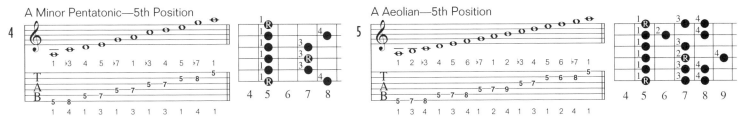

## Analysis

Unison bending, slides and awesome vibrato are key ingredients of a Jimmy Page solo. Page is a master of establishing an idea and building on it. He often outlines the chords using cleverly placed chord tones and arpeggios. He also extends ideas by repeating notable intervals or the rhythm of the initial idea.

This solo opens up with a common rock lick that includes a bend followed by a cascade of sixteenth notes. This flows nicely into the next bar where the note C (the 5th of the chord) is emphasized over the F chord. Bar 4 repeats the motif from bar 2, keeping the "story-line" of the solo easy to follow.

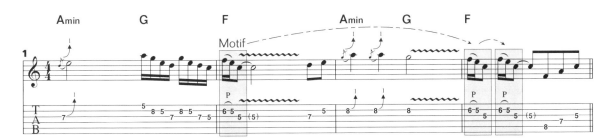

**Bar 5** contains an effective melodic idea using only two notes. The A note is played over the Amin chord, which is then bent up a whole step to B (3rd of the G chord).

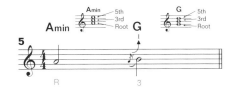

**Bars 9–12** build on an ascending melody using bends. Notice that the *target notes* (notes of arrival that are preceded by non-chord tones) are chord tones.

**Bars 13–15** have a climactic effect using an ascending flurry of sixteenth notes outlining each chord. Notice how the idea stays on the 2nd and 3rd strings.

## The Style of David Gilmour

The melodic guitar soloing of David Gilmour is nothing short of beautiful. Pink Floyd is well known for spacey, flowing and laid-back musical compositions. Their psychedelic rock, flavored with blues and R&B grooves, just begs for melodic and soulful solos. Gilmour shines on both. The following solo is in the style of Gilmour's rock ballad soloing.

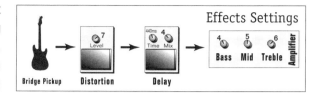

*Effects Settings*

*Dull the Pain*

**With Solo, Track 6**
**Backing Track, Track 7**

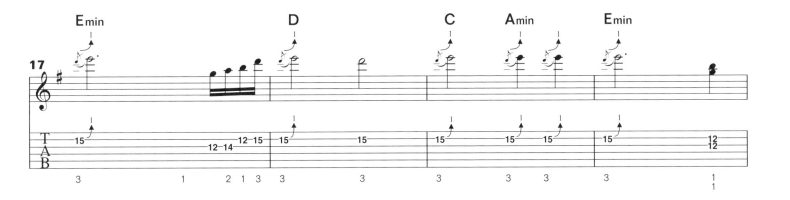

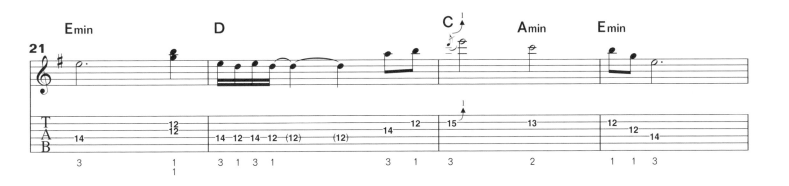

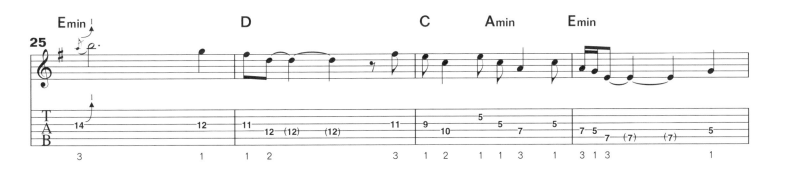

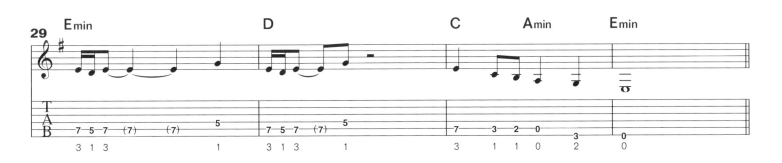

## The Chords and Scales

### The Chords
E Minor is the key center of this solo. The four-measure form follows a i–♭VII–VI–iv–i progression. Notice that the first and fourth measures are Emin, heavily emphasizing the key center. Familiarize yourself with the chords and their corresponding chord tones below, as David Gilmour's style of soloing uses chord tones extensively.

### The Scales
E Minor Pentatonic and E Aeolian are the scales used in this solo. Compare the notes in the chords with the notes in the scales. Notice that all the notes of the following scales are contained in the four chords above.

## Analysis

This solo is based mostly on melodic motifs, using chord tones and *scale fragments* (small portions of scale fingerings). Gilmour's phrasing in a ballad context is widely spaced and simple. This approach is very effective for beautiful, melodic soloing.

The first four measures use a fragment from the E Minor Pentatonic scale in 8th position. In **bars 1–3**, the notes are played in an order that creates a melody, targeting chord tones.

**Bars 5–8** maintain the vibe of the opening of the solo, primarily using notes from the E Minor Pentatonic scale in 5th position.

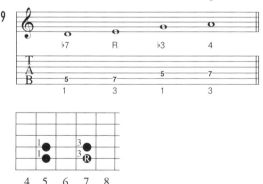

E Minor Pentatonic: 2nd and 3rd Strings

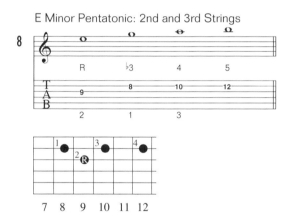

E Minor Pentatonic: 4th and 5th String

Arpeggios and triad fragments outline the chords in **bars 9–12**.

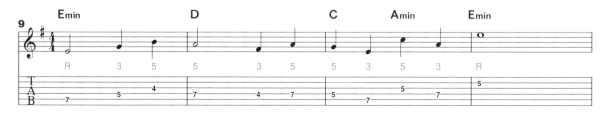

**Bars 13–15** are made of a single-string ascending line based on a bending idea. Notice that each bent note is a chord tone. **Bar 16** finishes the idea with an Minor Pentatonic lick in 12th position.

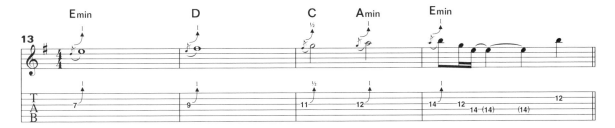

E Minor Pentatonic licks in 12th position continue through **bars 17–24**, cleverly hitting chord tones as the chords change, thus outlining the progression.

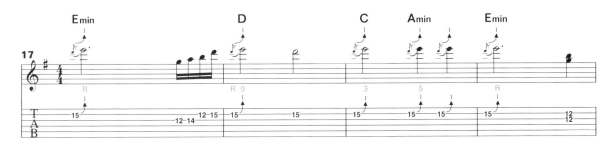

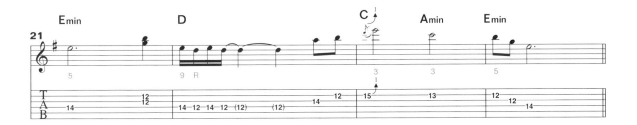

The last **8 bars (25–32)** are nothing more than descending melodic ideas, using E Minor Pentatonic with a small dose of E Aeolian.

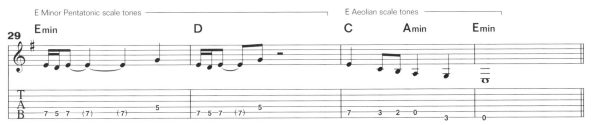

## The Style of Jeff Beck

Take the groove and the feel of blues, add some jazzy phrasing yet keep the energy of rock, and you have the guitar style of Jeff Beck. For this reason, Beck's style has often been classified as *fusion*. His soloing is very experimental and intense. He has no fear of playing a set of pentatonic rock licks over any chord, not letting any note or phrase go unturned.

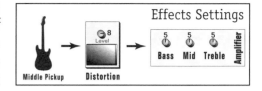

The following solo is played over a *shuffle* groove. A shuffle groove is one with a triplet feel, where *swing 8ths* are used (that is, the eighth notes are played in a long–short, long–short manner).

**With Solo, Track 8**
**Backing Track, Track 9**

## Traffic Jam

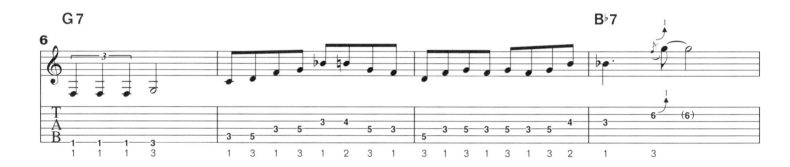

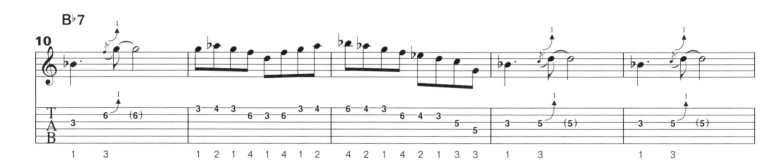

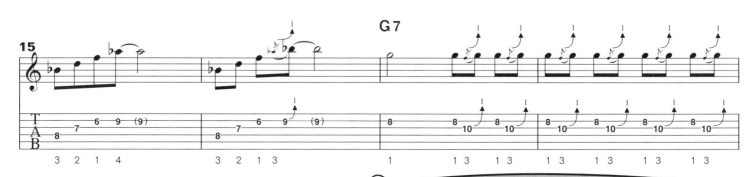

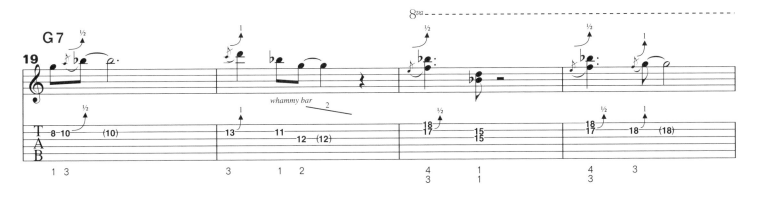

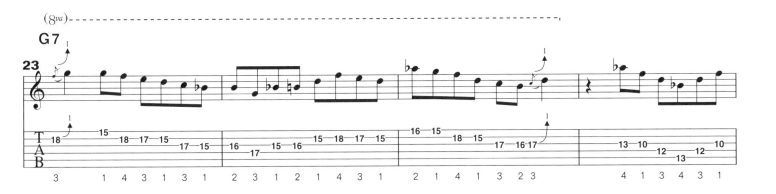

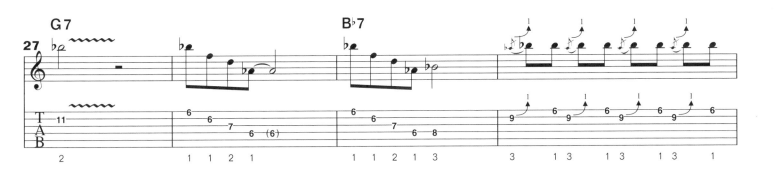

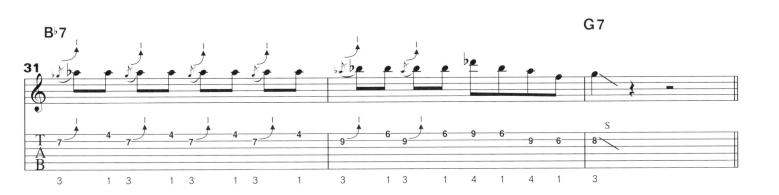

## The Chords and Scales

### The Chords

There are only two chords in this tune: G7 and B♭7. Think of each chord as I7. The interval between the roots of the two chords is a minor 3rd.

### The Scales

With both chords in the progression being thought of as I7, each chord is its own key. The scales that fit the G7 chord best are:

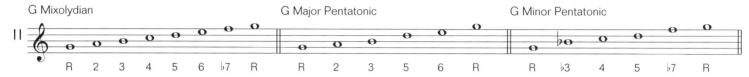

In rock soloing, it's very common to use a minor pentatonic scale over a dominant chord even though the chord has a major 3rd while the scale contains a minor 3rd. This clash has become an acceptable, even expected, part of the blues and blues-rock sound. The G Minor Pentatonic scale can be played over the G7 chord. It can also be mixed with the G Mixolydian and G Major Pentatonic scales in the same context.

Use the following scales over the B♭7 chord.

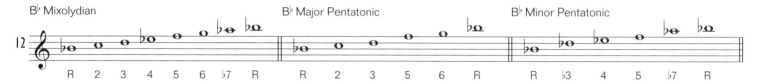

## Analysis

The opening is a *calling* motif (the first part of a call and response phrase) using the notes of the G Minor Pentatonic scale. Notice the idea begins on the second beat. **Bars 3–4** include a great example of mixing the minor 3rd (B♭) and the major 3rd (B) from the major and minor pentatonic scales.

**Bars 5–8** continue the opening theme. **Bar 6** has a cool *tension and release* idea using the ♭7 (F) and the root (G) set to a quarter-note triplet rhythm, while **bars 7–8** mix the minor and major pentatonic scales once again. Tension is created when an unstable note or non-chord tone—a *dissonance* (clashing sound)—is played by the soloist against the chord. This tension is released when that note moves to a more stable note or one that is contained in the same chord or a chord that follows—a *consonance* (harmonious sound). In this case, ♭7 is less stable than the root.

The B♭7 chord makes a surprising entrance at **bar 9** after eight measures of G7. **Bars 9–10** and **13–14** are the call, while **bars 11–12** and **15–16** are the response. The Mixolydian scale is used in **bars 11–12**. A B♭7 arpeggio is used over **bars 15–16**.

The G7 chord comes back in **bar 17**, where there are repeated minor pentatonic bending licks. The *double-stop* (two notes played simultaneously) ideas in **bar 21–22** are created from the G Minor Pentatonic scale.

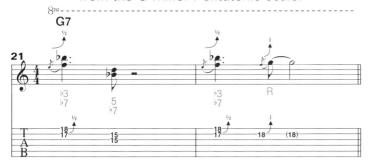

A final run over the B♭7 in **bar 25** serves up a blend of B♭ Mixolydian mode and B♭ Major Pentatonic scale. The B♭7 arpeggio licks in **bars 26–29** and bluesy unison bends on **bars 30–32** are drawn from the B♭ Minor Pentatonic scale.

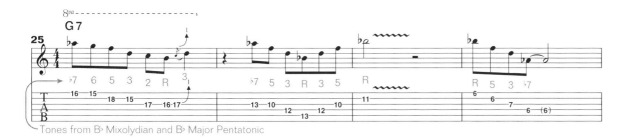

**CHAPTER 2**

## The Rock Style of Jimi Hendrix

Jimi Hendrix was one of the most influential guitarists in rock music, which would sound much different today had Hendrix never come along. To this day, his influence can be heard in the playing of countless guitar players. At the time, his guitar soloing was like nothing anyone on the planet had ever experienced. Influenced by many blues players—along with the folk music of Bob Dylan—Hendrix took traditional guitar soloing to the next level and beyond. Hendrix's rock soloing style can be described in one word: aggressive. A "play-it-like-you-mean-it" delivery of the notes is key to achieving this often chaotic-sounding lead style. Hit the strings hard and use a wide vibrato.

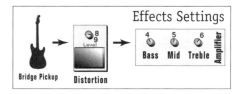

**With Solo, Track 10**
**Backing Track, Track 11**

### Don't Play with Matches

✕ = Muted note. A pitchless, percussive sound.

## The Chords and Scales

### The Chords

Although there are no chords being played, the implied harmonis are I–♭VII. There are two key centers in this solo. The bass guitar plays a line constructed from the D Blues scale in **bars 1–8**, and then moves up a whole step to E Blues for **bars 9–17**. Note that in **bars 1–8**, the chord changes really happen on the last eighth note of the measure. This is an *anticipation*, which is a move to a tone from the new chord before the written chord change—usually just before a bar line.

### The Scales

With only bass guitar in the accompaniment, there is no solid harmonic reference for the soloist. For this reason there are many scales that work well over the progression. Being heavily influenced by the blues, Hendrix made good use of minor pentatonic and blues scales. He often moves the same scale type from one key center to another. The scales used in the solo are:

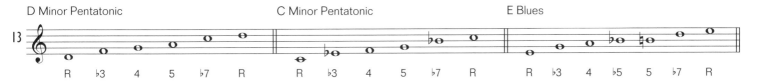

D Minor Pentatonic        C Minor Pentatonic        E Blues

You can add a ♭5 to any minor pentatonic scale to get the blues scale. Try this with the D Minor (add an A♭) and C Minor (add a G♭) Pentatonic scales.

## Analysis

The ♭7–R bends (C–D over the D and B♭–C over the C) in **bars 1–2** set up the main theme for this solo.

**Bars 3–4** continue on with a twist: the bent note (D) is released to C, thus matching the note played by the bass.

**Bar 5** has a double-stop bend, which is repeated without the bend in **bar 6**. The phrasing of the lick in these two measures synchronizes with the bass, outlining the changes.

**Bars 9–10** revisit the beginning of the solo using the same phrasing transposed up a whole step to E.

**Bar 11** contains a cool, rhythmic idea. Note the use of muted notes, indicated with the ✕ mark. These notes are executed by leaving your fingers on the strings but not pressing them to the fretboard, creating a pitchless, percussive sound.

The end (**bars 14–15**) is a descending E Minor Pentatonic scale, with a hint of the E Blues scale—because of the ♭5 (B♭)—in **bar 15**.

# The Blues Style of Jimi Hendrix

"Eat at Joe's" is an example of Hendrix's rock-blues style. This blues side of Jimi's soloing borrowed heavily from various blues masters, though he put his own stamp on it. This example makes extensive use of "call and response" phrasing (see page 7), which is used extensively in the blues.

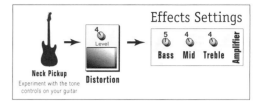

**With Solo, Track 12**
**Backing Track, Track 13**

## Eat at Joe's

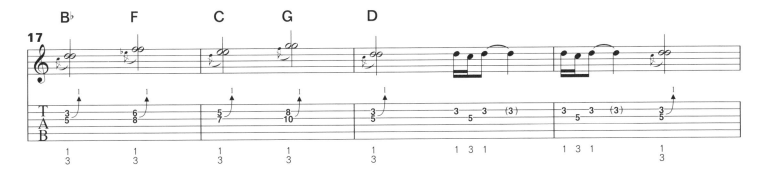

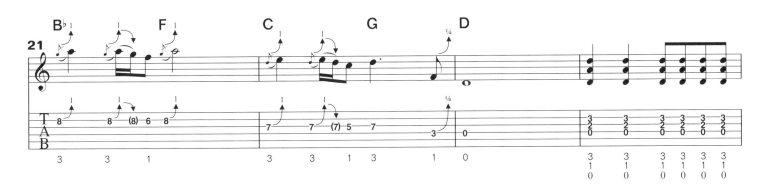

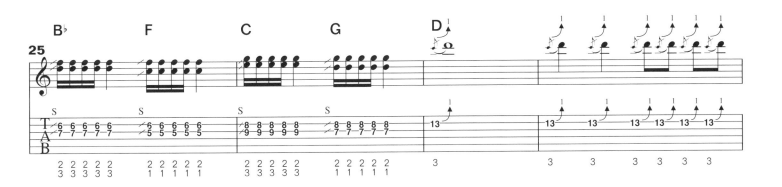

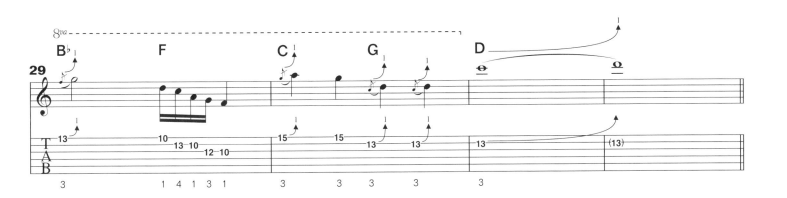

### The Chords and Scales

#### The Chords

This chord progression moves through three different key centers: **Bar 1** is a I–V in B♭, **bar 2** is a I–V in C. **Bars 3–4** rest on D. Notice that the roots all move up by a perfect 5th (or down by perfect 4th).

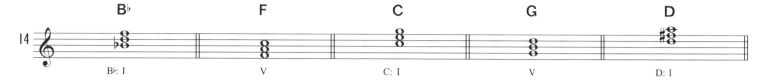

#### The Scales

As you learned on page 16, it is common to play minor pentatonic scales over major or dominant chords. This solo uses the same technique.

### Analysis

The first two measures start with a major pentatonic motif: B♭ Major Pentatonic over **bar 1** and C Major Pentatonic over **bar 2**. Single D notes are used over **bars 3–4**.

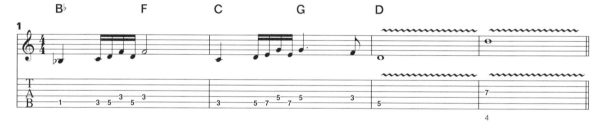

**Bars 5–6** maintain the opening theme by mimicking bars 1–2 up an octave. Sprinkles of D Minor Pentatonic in **bars 7–8** emphasize the root D.

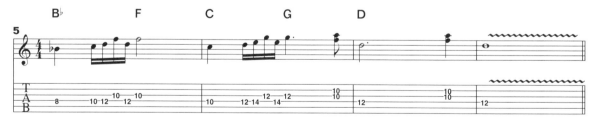

D Minor Pentatonic is played in both **bars 9 and 10**.

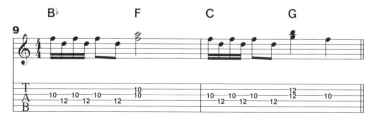

**Bars 13–14** continue with the D Minor Pentatonic scale that flows into a bending phrase over the D chord in **bars 15–16**. The bend targets the note A, which is the 5th of the D chord.

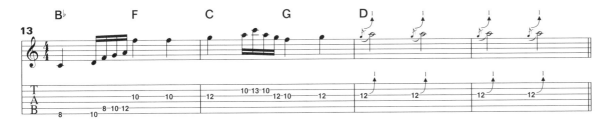

Unison bends in **bars 17–18** cleverly highlight chord tones in sync with the rhythm of the chords.

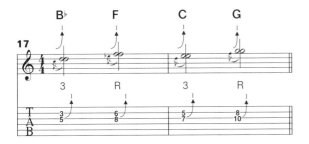

**Bars 25–26** contain a nice series of double stops that are derived from, and move with, the chords.

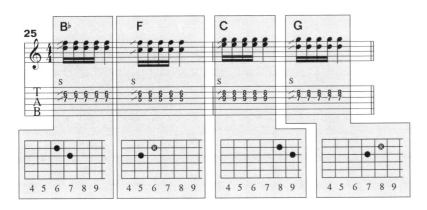

A long, gradual bend from the ♭7 (C) to the root (D) creates a captivating ending by slowly resolving tension.

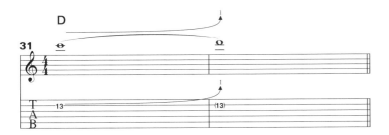

# The Ballad Style of Jimi Hendrix

Although most of Hendrix's soloing style is melodic, this characteristic really shines in his ballad style. "An Angel Gets Her Wings" contains vocal-style melodies that are emotional and memorable. Other hallmarks of this style include sliding double stops and the liberal use of chord embellishments.

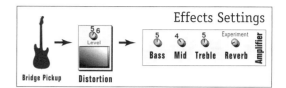

**With Solo, Track 14**
**Backing Track, Track 15**

## *An Angel Gets Her Wings*

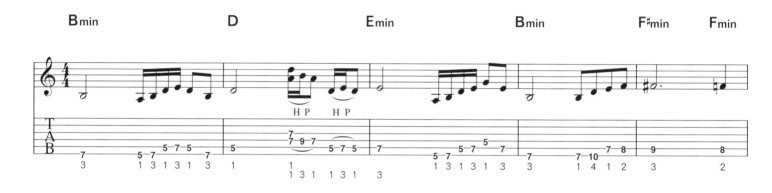

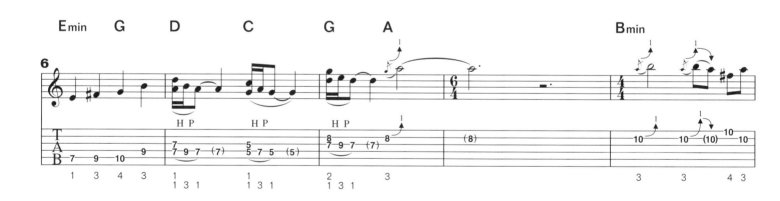

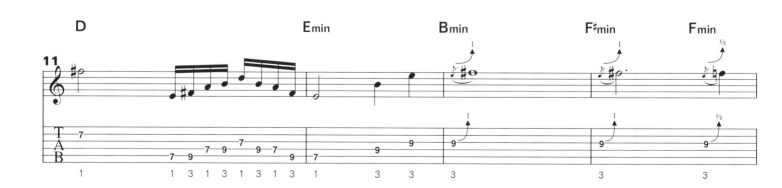

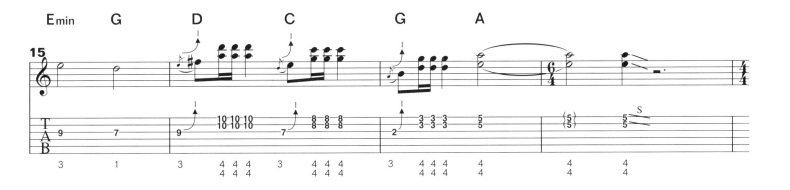

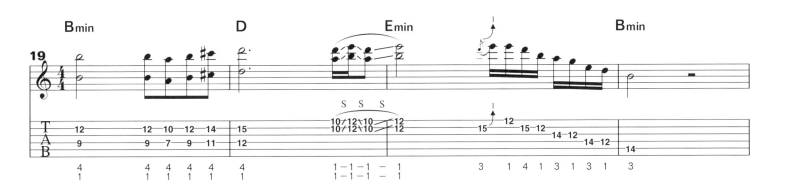

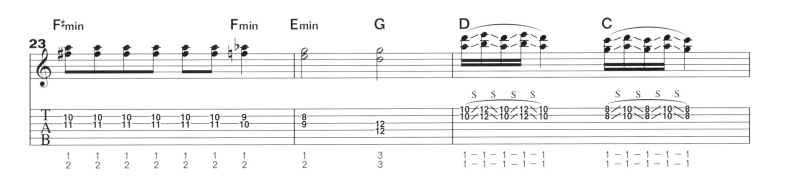

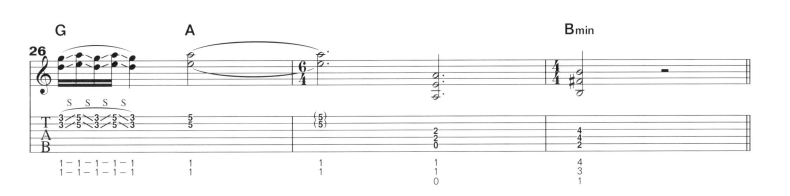

### The Chords and Scales

#### The Chords

B Minor is the primary key center of this ballad. The progression is eight bars long with a $\frac{6}{4}$ measure tacked on every ninth bar. There is a *chromatic passing chord* (a non-diatonic chord that comes between two diatonic chords in the progression) in **bar 5** of the progression. The chords are i, III, iv, v, ♭v, v, VI, although there is a temporary shift to G (V–IV) in **bar 7**. B Minor returns in (VI–♭VII) in **bar 8**.

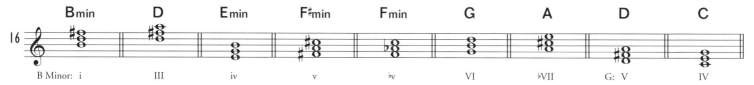

#### The Scales

Here are the scales used in this solo:

### Analysis

**Bars 1–4** set up the theme of the entire solo. As each new chord is played, the root of that chord is played in the solo. The same ideas is used in **bars 5–8**. In **bars 2, 7 and 8**, double-stop embellishments using hammer-ons and pull-offs are used to outline the chords.

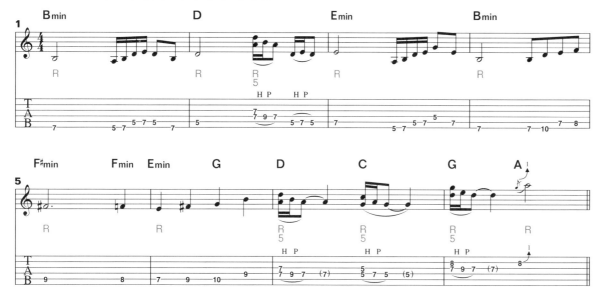

**Bars 10–14** use B Minor Pentatonic at the 7th position. The phrasing of each measure sets up a targeted chord tone for the following measure. This is a great soloing technique for *making the changes* (reflecting the chord changes in a solo).

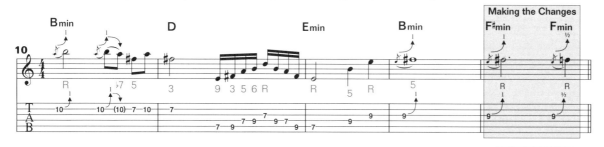

**Bars 16–17** serve up a nice descending bend and double-stop lick that outlines the chords.

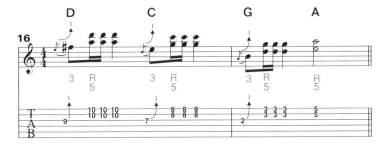

An octave motif is introduced in **bar 19**, which is followed by sliding double stops in perfect 4ths. E Minor Pentatonic is used over the Emin chord in **bar 21**.

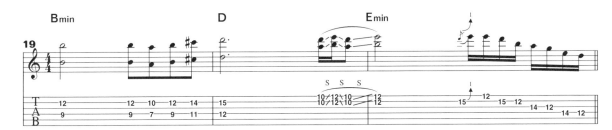

The solo finishes over **bars 23–26** with more double stops that outline the chords.

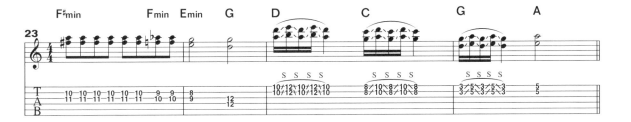

# CHAPTER 3

## The Dorian Mode

The Dorian mode, which is the second mode of the major scale, is a minor mode (it has a minor 3rd, $\flat$3). Many great players, including Carlos Santana, Eric Johnson and Ty Tabor (Kings X), use this mode frequently. The Dorian mode can be thought of as a major scale with a $\flat$3 and $\flat$7, or a natural minor scale with a raised 6th. When combined with the minor pentatonic scale built on the same root, the Dorian mode adds some spice. The following solo has a Latin-rock feel, in which the Dorian flavor fits well.

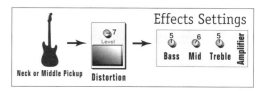

**With Solo, Track 16**
**Backing Track, Track 17**

### Hot Sauce

## The Chords and Scales

### The Chords

This solo is in D Minor (Dorian). A typical minor chord progression in rock would be i–iv, which is an Aeolian progression (the iv chord in the Aeolian mode is minor). The chord progression for this solo is a two-chord vamp, i–IV. The major IV chord makes Dorian's sound unique.

### The Scales

Here are the scales used in the solo. Notice that all of the notes in the minor pentatonic scale are also in the Dorian mode.

Notice that the notes in D Dorian are the same as those for the C Major scale, beginning and ending on D, which is why it is called a "mode" of the major scale.

## Analysis

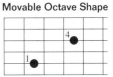

Movable Octave Shape

This solo begins with sliding octaves on the 5th and 3rd strings.

In **bars 1–2**, a nice melodic motif is set up using mostly chord tones over the D Minor chord.

In **bars 3–4**, the theme is continued over the G chord. In **bar 4**, a nice ascending melody is established which lands on the G octave—the root of the chord.

In **bars 5–8**, the idea from bars **1–4** is carried over, now with descending sliding octaves on the 4th and 2nd strings. Notice that the octave lick in **bar 6** emphasizes the 5th of the chord (A) and the B brings out the Dorian flavor (it is the major 6th of the mode, another of its distinguishing features). The same phrase is used in **bar 8** over the G chord, only this time the root of the chord is being targeted along with the F, which adds a dominant flavor to the G chord (F is the ♭7).

**Bar 9** begins with a whole-step bend then continues into a descending minor 7–arpeggio lick. A G7 arpeggio idea continues in **bar 11**, ending with a G double stop. The final licks in **bars 13–17** of the solo use the D Dorian mode in 10th position.

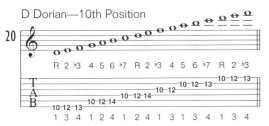

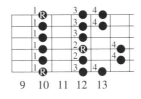

Dmin7 Arpeggio

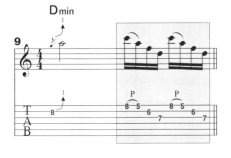

# The Phrygian Mode

If you favor a haunting, mysterious sound, then Phrygian is the mode for you. It is a minor scale that is often thought of as having a Spanish sound. Players from many styles, from the metal of Marty Friedman to the jazz of Al Di Meola, favor the Phrygian mode. Many hard rock bands use it because of its dark and heavy effect. The Phrygian mode is the third mode of the major scale. For example, E Phrygian is the C Major scale beginning and ending on E. You can also think of this mode as the Aeolian mode with a ♭2. "Zorro's Mask" is a prime example of the Phrygian experience.

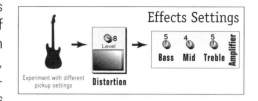

## Zorro's Mask

**With Solo, Track 18**
**Backing Track, Track 19**

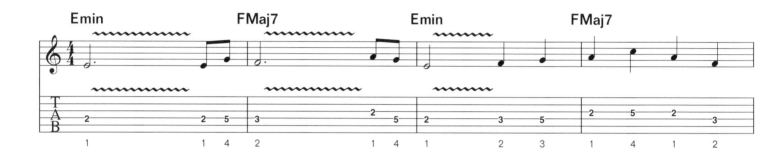

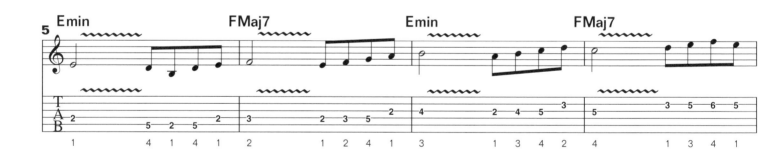

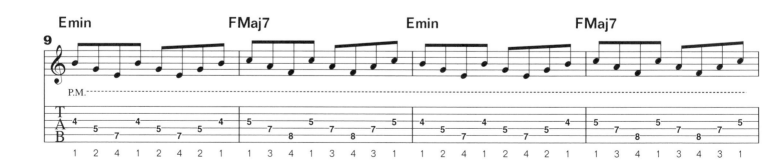

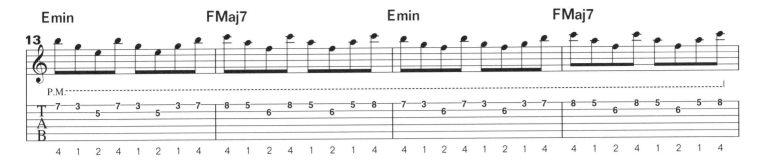

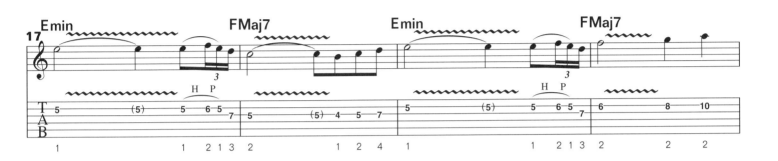

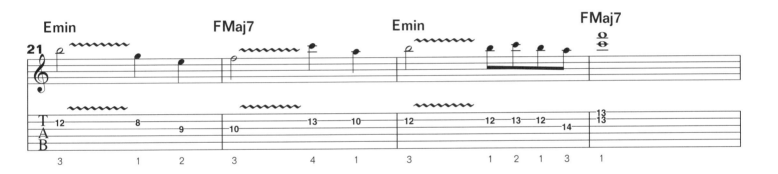

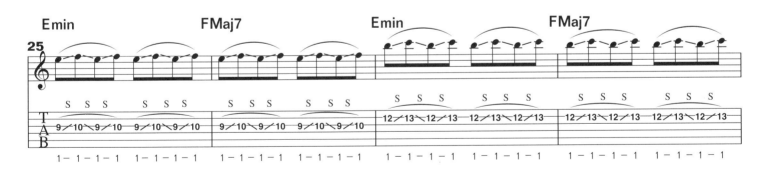

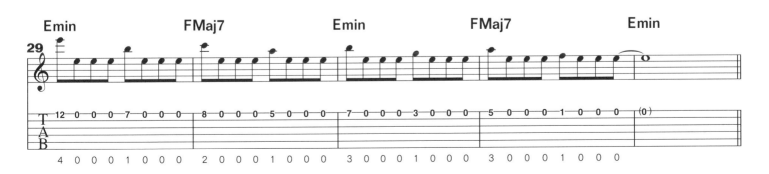

## The Chords and Scales

E Minor to F Major 7 is a perfect Phrygian chord progression. The back-and-forth half-step movement of the chords creates a somber effect. The key is E Minor (Phrygian).

### The Chords

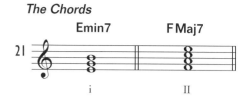

### The Scale

Here is the E Phrygian mode as used in the solo.

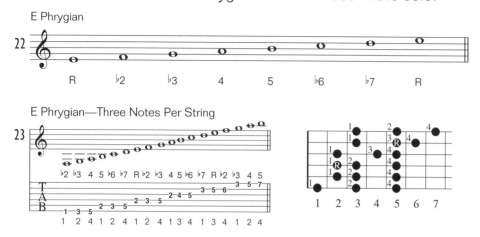

Below are two arpeggio shapes used in this solo.

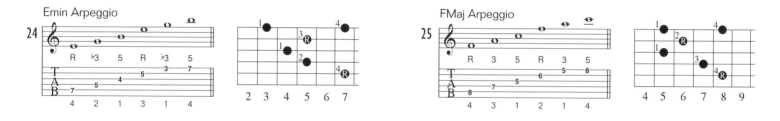

## Analysis

**Bars 1–4** are composed mostly of chord tones.

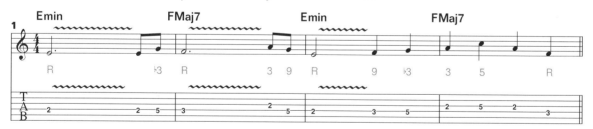

**Bars 5–8** continue with chord tones, intensifying the notes with added embellishments. Notice the rhythmic consistency.

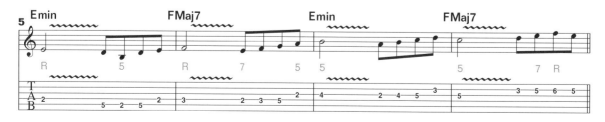

**Bars 9–16** introduce palm-muted arpeggios in steady eighth notes. In **bars 9–12**, the arpeggio is played in a consistent pattern in the lower octave. The same arpeggio sequence is played in the higher octave in **bars 13–16**.

**Bars 17–20** build on a motif targeting chord tones, once again keeping the rhythm consistent and easy to follow.

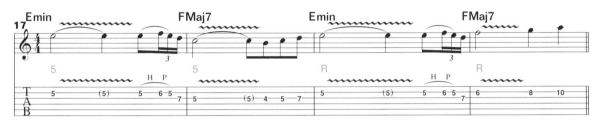

**In bars 25–26**, the melody slides back and forth in half-step motion between E and F. **Bars 27–28** use the same back and forth pattern between B and C.

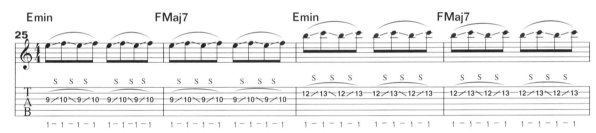

This solo ends using a very Spanish-sounding single-string lick alternating between fretted chord tones from the E Phrygian mode and the open string.

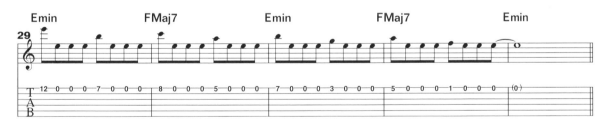

E Phrygian—Single String

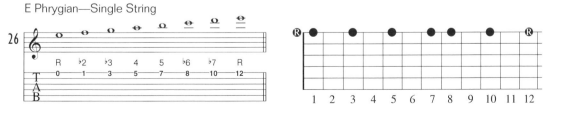

The Lydian mode is very bright and uplifting. Joe Satriani and Steve Vai use the Lydian mode to their music. Lydian is the fourth mode of the major scale and can be thought of as a major scale with a #4. In this solo, the light, airy sound of the Lydian mode creates a pop-rock feel.

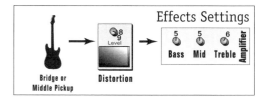

## 4th Degree

With Solo, Track 20
Backing Track, Track 21

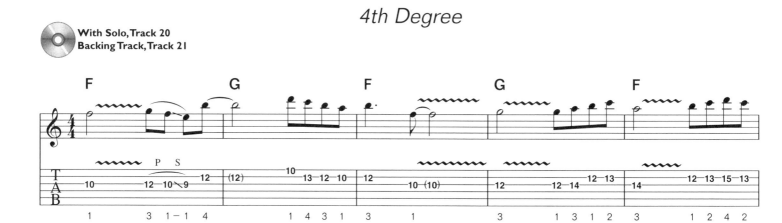

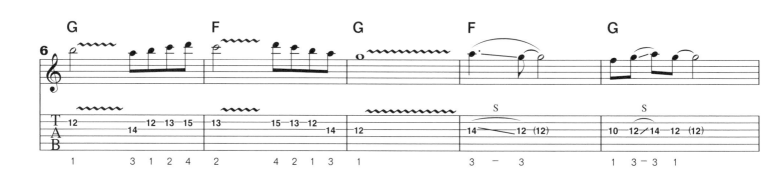

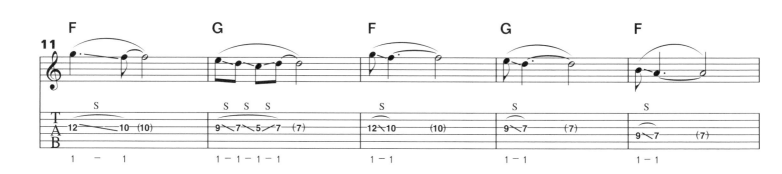

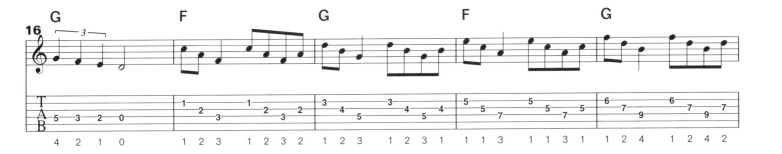

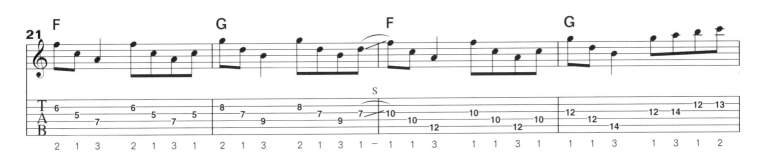

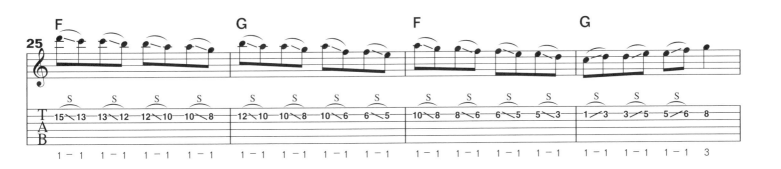

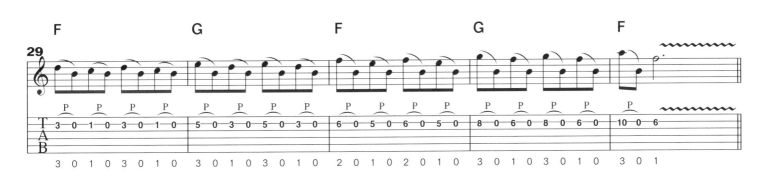

## The Chords and Scales

This solo is in F Major (Lydian). The progression is a two-chord vamp: F and G. It is important to note that the bass guitar plays steady eighth notes on F for the entire solo, keeping the focus on the F Lydian sound. The notes of each chord are spelled out below.

*The Chords*

The notes in F Lydian are the same as the notes in C Major, beginning and ending on F.

## Analysis

This solo begins in **bars 1–4** with licks built from the F Lydian mode in the 10th position. Strong emphasis is placed on the F and B notes, which are the distinguishing features of the scale.

F Lydian—One Octave, 10th Position

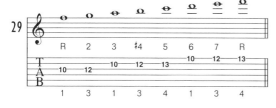
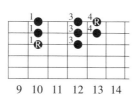

**Bars 5–8** continue in the character of the opening, but in the 12th position (first appears in bar 4).

F Lydian—One Octave, 12th Position

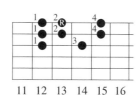

A nice melodic idea that uses slides on a single string appears in **bars 9–14**.

F Lydian—Single-String Slides

**31**
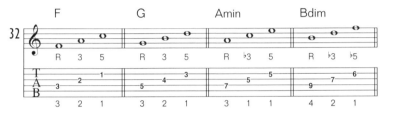
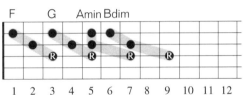

Triads are outlined in **bars 17–24**. The Amin arpeggio is played over the F chord, creating an FMaj7 sound. The Bdim arpeggio is palyed over the G chord, creating a G7 sound.

**32**

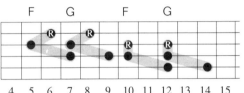

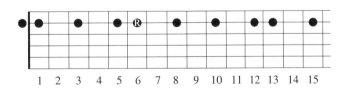

A single-string lick appears in **bar 25–33**, first with slides, then with a combination of pull-offs to the open 2nd string.

F Lydian—Single String

**33**

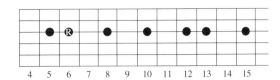

## The Mixolydian Mode

If you want to add a rock edge to your blues playing (or vice versa), the Mixolydian mode will do the trick. Billy Gibbons (ZZ Top), Dave Davies (The Kinks) and Pete Townshend (The Who) embellish their rock solos with a taste of the blues, using the Mixolydian mode. Mixolydian is the fifth mode of the major scale, and can be thought of as a major scale with a ♭7, which is why it works well over dominant 7th chords.

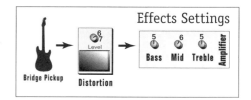

*Effects Settings*

## Mixo-ing It Up

**With Solo, Track 22**
**Backing Track, Track 23**

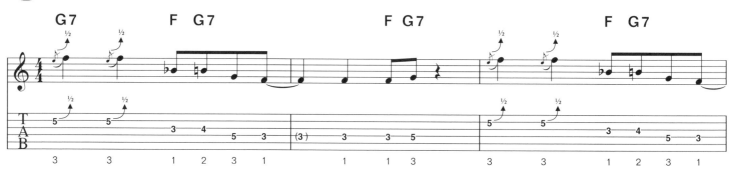

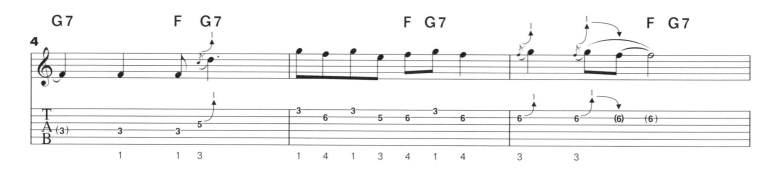

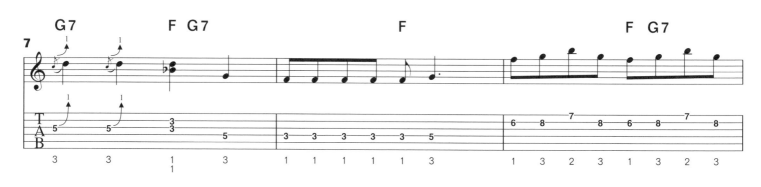

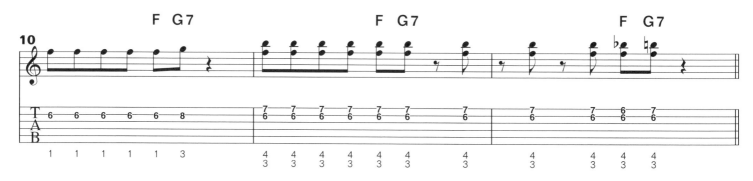

## The Chords and Scales

The key center of this 12-bar solo is G Mixolydian. The progression is best thought of as I7–♭VII, grooving mostly on the G7 chord.

*The Chords*

*The Scales*

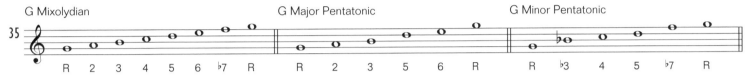

The notes in the G Mixolydian mode are the same as those in the C Major scale, beginning and ending on the fifth note (G). When soloing over this type of rock/blues riff, it is common to mix major and minor pentatonic scales.

## Analysis

**Bar 1** starts with a half-step bend that accents the F (♭7), which is the distinguising characteristic of the G Mixolydian mode. The F is also the ♭7 of the G7 chord. The lick continues by mixing the G Major Pentatonic and G Minor Pentatonic scales into a G Major/Minor Pentatonic Composite scale.

G Major/Minor Pentatonic Composite

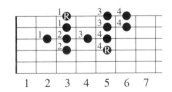

# CHAPTER 4

## The Style of Neal Schon

Soulful and melodic: These two words best describe Neal Schon's guitar solos. Schon began playing with the legendary Carlos Santana at the tender age of 15. He took this influence with him and brought Journey to popularity. Schon is a master of melody and embellishment as is another of his major influences, Jeff Beck.

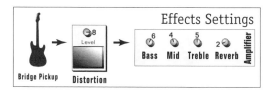

Effects Settings

*Drive-Thru Order*

With Solo, Track 24
Backing Track, Track 25

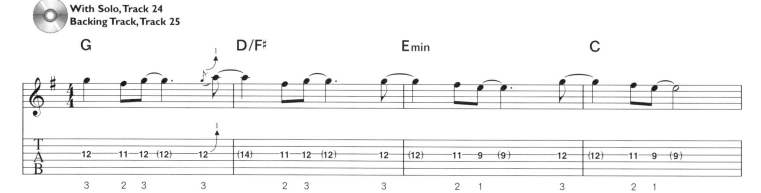

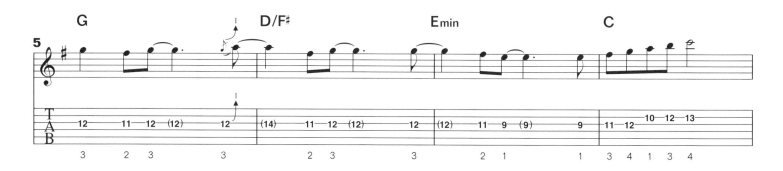

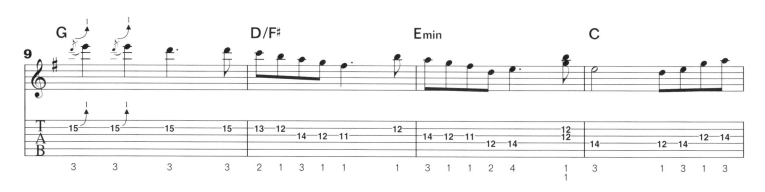

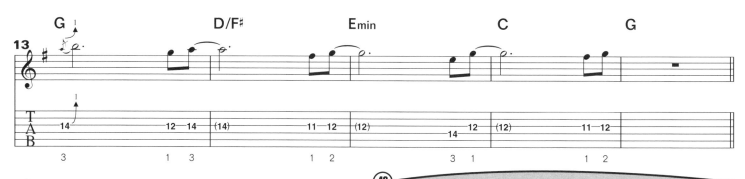

## The Chords and Scales

This pop chord progression is a I–V–vi–IV in the key of G.

### The Chords

### The Scales

## Analysis

**Bars 1–8** open with a simple melody that uses the G Major scale. Take note of how the first seven bars are created from a three-note rhythmic motif that is presented in the first measure and later varied with anticipations. This melodic approach is very effective for unifying your solo.

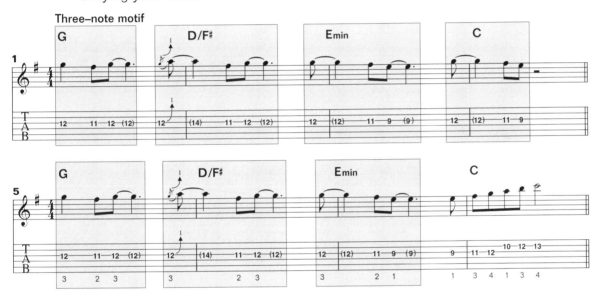

**Bars 9–12** provide a contrast to the opening theme. **Bars 9–11** use a linear fragment from the G Major scale while **bar 12** uses a small pattern from the G Major Pentatonic in 12th position.

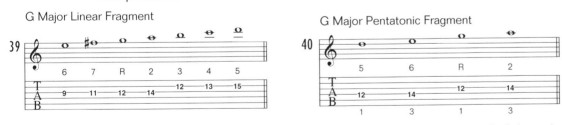

A slightly modified version of the original motif returns for the end of the solo in **bars 13–16**; the first note in the three-note motive is lengthened. This return to a previous idea ties the solo together and makes it more memorable.

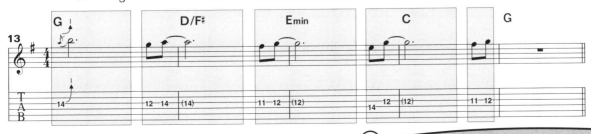

## The Style of Tom Scholz

Believe it or not, Boston's Tom Scholz didn't even pick up his first guitar until he was 21. Scholz never expected to become famous, but has become widely known for his harmonized lead lines. While playing the guitar as a hobby, he encountered the work of Jimmy Page, Jeff Beck and Eric Clapton. Scholz became an influential guitarist by honing his talents as a song-writer, producer and recording engineer. He also played nearly every instrument on Boston's self-titled debut album.

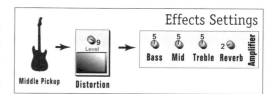

## Brain Mass

**With Solo, Track 26**
**Backing Track, Track 27**

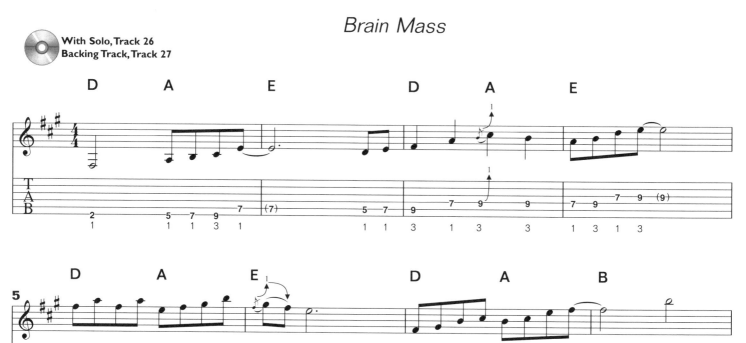

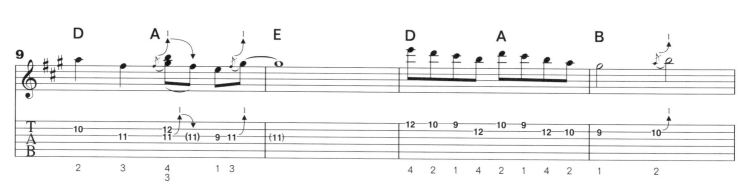

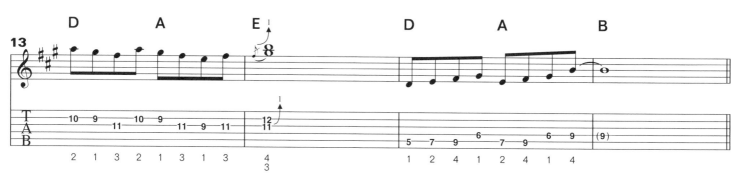

## The Chords and Scales

Although the chords in this solo come from the key of A Major, the key center is E. Since E is the fifth note of the A Major scale, this is a Mixolydian chord progression.

*The Chords*

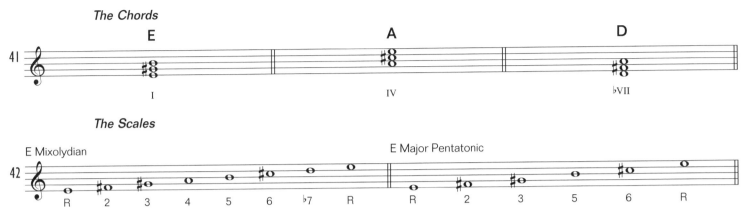

*The Scales*

E Mixolydian                                                E Major Pentatonic

42

R  2  3  4  5  6  ♭7  R        R  2  3  5  6  R

## Analysis

**Bar 1** begins with a low F♯ held over the D chord. A smooth, ascending E Major Pentatonic lick follows in **bar 2**, landing on the root of the E chord.

**Bars 3–4** continue up the fretboard, outlining the chords along the way.

The major pentatonic scale is used in **bars 5–8**, outlining the chords once again.

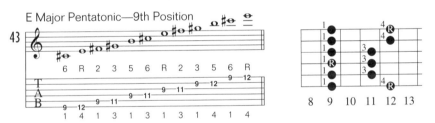

A sweet-sounding major pentatonic idea is played over **bar 9**.

The E Mixolydian mode appears in **bar 11** mixed with major pentatonic fragments.

**Bar 13** sets up a double-stop bend in **bar 14**. The last phrase begins in **bar 15**, combining the Mixolydian mode and major pentatonic scale.

## The Style of The Eagles

The Eagles burst onto the music scene in the early 1970s with a folk and pop-rock sound that was perfect for FM radio. Guitarists Joe Walsh and Don Felder played beautiful solos, which typically included tasteful pentatonic and arpeggio licks. They would often play two-guitar, harmonized solos (see pages 76–77 for another harmony solo). The following solo is a prime example of their harmonized guitar solo technique.

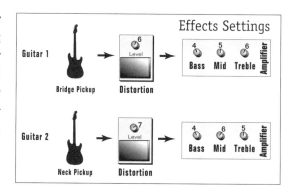

## West Coast Lodging

**With Solo, Track 28**
**Backing Track, Track 29**

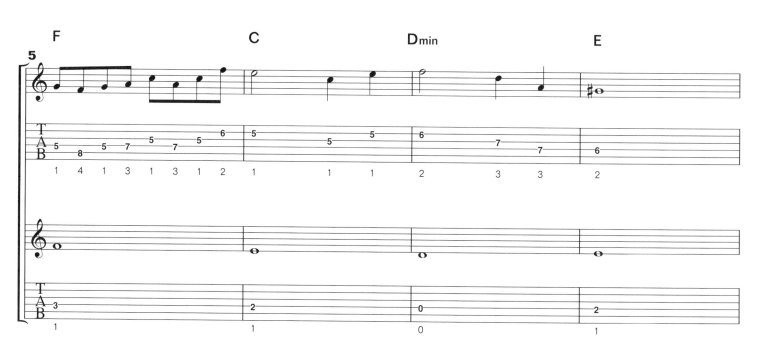

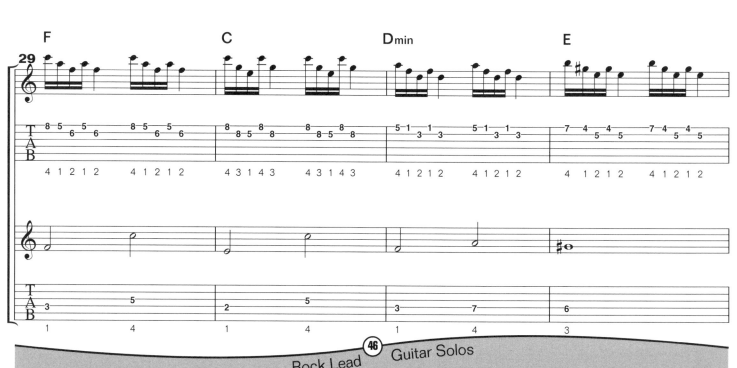

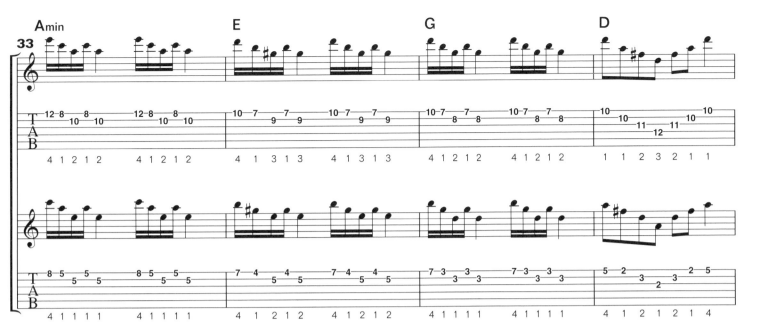

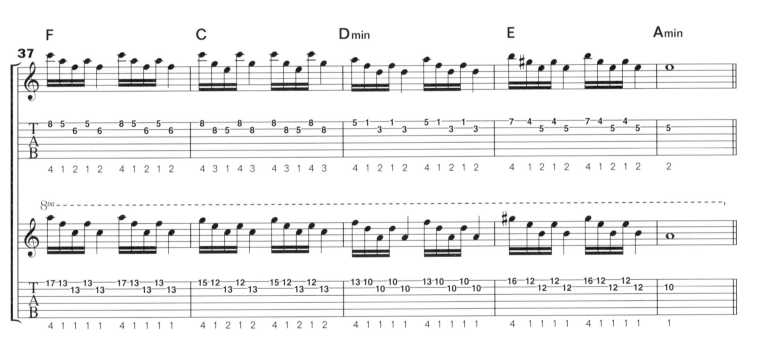

## The Chords and Scales

The chord progression in this solo moves through three key centers: A, G and F. The progression is as follows: i–V in A Minor, I–V in G Major, I–V in F Major, and iv–V in A Minor.

### The Chords

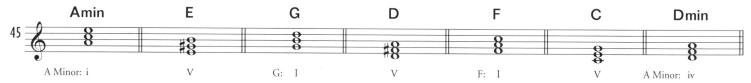

### The Scales

The first half of the solo uses these scales.

There is also frequent use of arpeggios in this solo, especially in the second half.

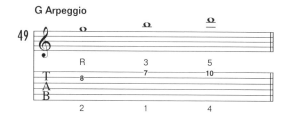

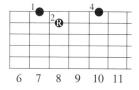

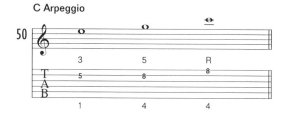

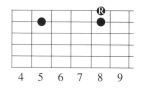

## Analysis

This solo features a harmony guitar part. In **bars 1–16**, Guitar 1 plays the main solo. Guitar 2 plays a very simple melody that reflects the underlying chord structure.

In **bars 17–24** and **33–41**, Guitar 2 plays in harmony with Guitar 1 in exactly the same rhythm. For this solo to work, Guitar 2 must lock in perfectly with Guitar 1. In **bars 17–24**, Guitar 2 is higher than Guitar 1. In **bars 33–25** Guitar 1 is higher than Guitar 2. All of the harmonized notes are diatonic; the 3rds can be major or minor, depending on the notes of the chord over which they are played. Sometimes, the guitars are harmonizing in 4ths (for example, the quarter notes in bars 33, 35, 37 and so on).

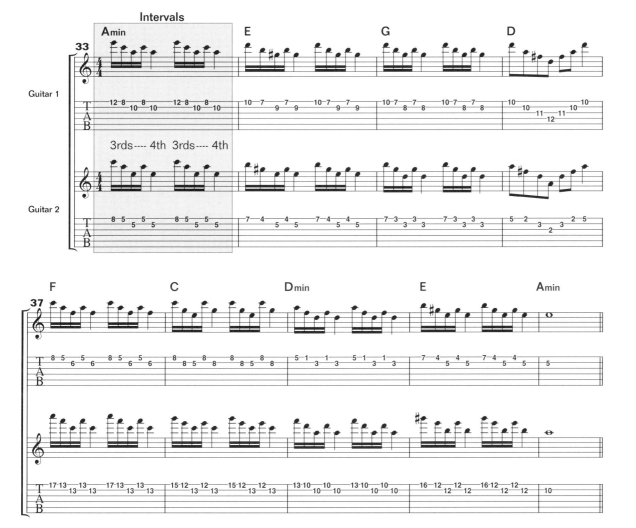

If you are going to be playing Guitar 2, it is beneficial to first learn Guitar 1, then learn the harmony part. This will allow you to visualize how the two parts lie on the fretboard. Examine both parts one measure at a time and observe the chords both guitars are arpeggiating. This process will help you understand the technique so that you can begin harmonizing your own solos.

When the twang of the country guitar meets the hard edge of the rock lead guitar, you get Southern rock. Lynyrd Skynyrd, ZZ Top, Molly Hatchet and Creedence Clearwater Revival—to name a few—mixed this recipe to produce rock solos that have claimed their spot in music history.

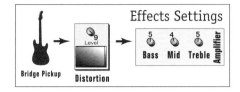

## Southern Junction Jamming

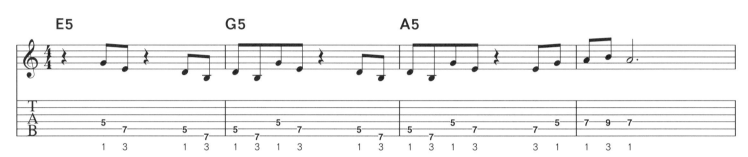

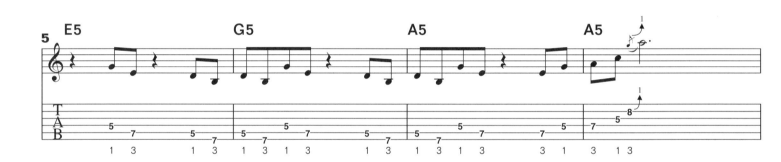

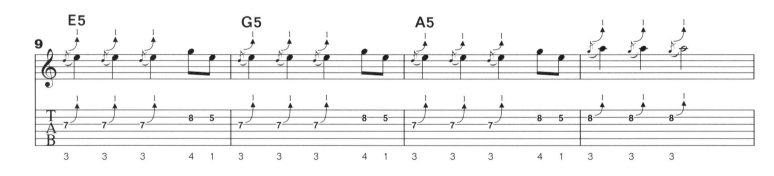

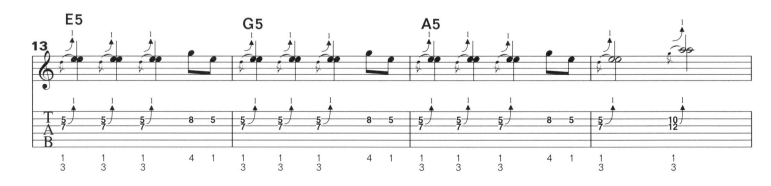

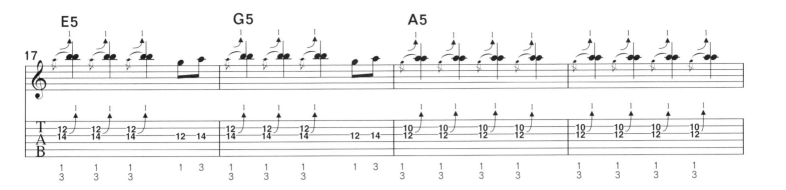

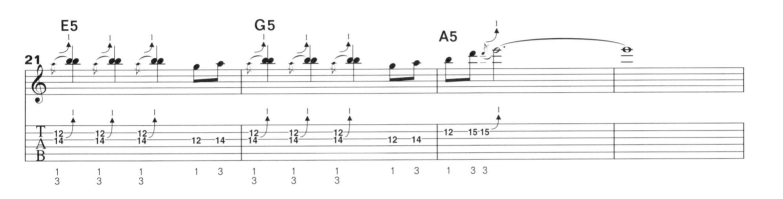

## The Chords and Scales

This down-home, rockin' solo is in E Minor. The progression is i–III–iv and uses the power chords E5, G5 and A5. This progression is very common in Southern and hard rock styles.

*The Chords*

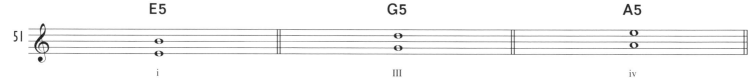

*The Scales*

The E Minor Pentatonic scale works well with this chord progression.

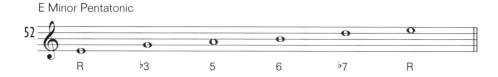

Compare the notes in the scale with the notes in the chords. Every note in the scale fits the chords perfectly.

## Analysis

Notice that this 32-bar solo is based on licks that are repeated over 8-bar passages. In each passage, the first bar introduces a motif which is repeated in the following six bars. The last bar of each passage is an ending of the idea. This type of *motivic* soloing is very common in Southern rock, and makes the extended solos that southern rock bands are known for possible.

The repeated idea using low notes from the E Minor Pentatonic scale in 5th position in **bars 1–8** make for a gritty opening. **Bar 8** ends the passage with a whole-step bend to the A note over the A5 chord.

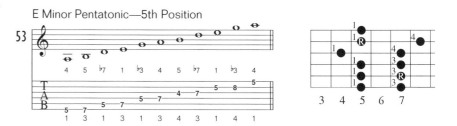

**Bars 9–16** use bends in the 5th position. **Bars 9–12** use a single-string bend, while **bars 13–16** use unison bends.

The unison bend motif continues through **bars 17–22**, finishing with a whole-step bend up to the E note over the A5 chord in **bars 23–24**.

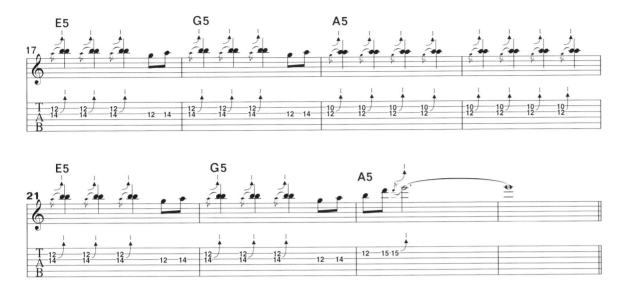

**Bars 25–26** use a double stop idea, while **bars 27–28** feature a Chuck Berry–inspired lick. The solo finishes with a climactic ending that uses a repeated pull-off lick in **bars 29–32**.

## The Style of Ritchie Blackmore

Ritchie Blackmore began his contributions to rock guitar in the mid 1960s, but is best known for the unique soloing style from his years with Deep Purple. Blackmore incorporates his admiration of The Who with his love for the drama found in the classical music of Vivaldi and J.S. Bach. This quasi-classical approach pioneered a new style of soloing, paving the way for a new generation of guitarists to freely explore beyond the boundaries of the typical rock guitar solo.

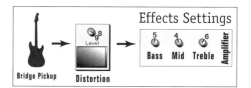

*High-Test Octane*

**With Solo, Track 32**
**Backing Track, Track 33**

Rock Lead Guitar Solos

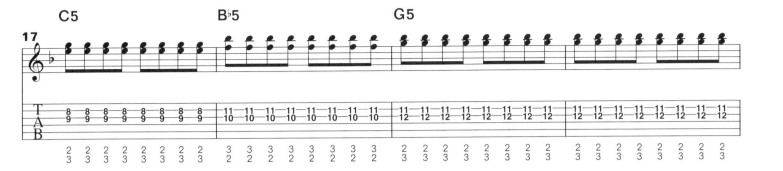

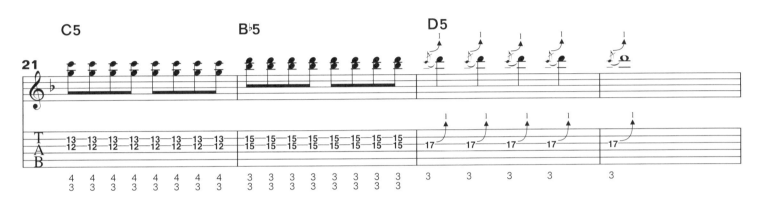

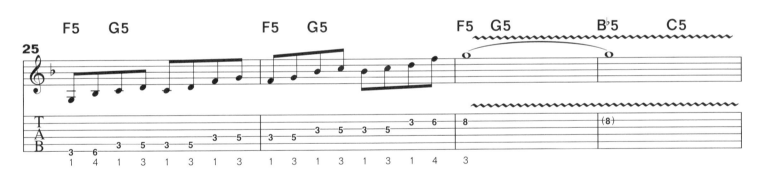

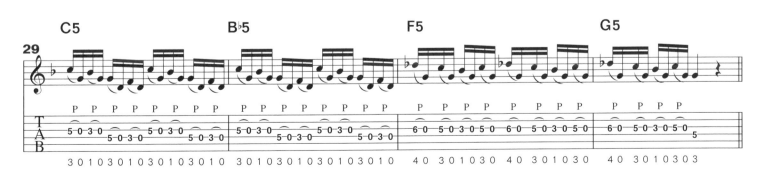

## The Chords and Scales

The chords in this solo are the power chords F5, G5, B♭5, C5 and D5. The key center is G.

Here are the notes that make up each chord.

*The Chords*

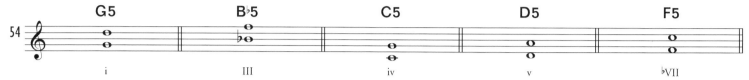

| G5 | B♭5 | C5 | D5 | F5 |
|----|-----|----|----|-----|
| i | III | iv | v | ♭VII |

*The Scales*

G Aeolian, G Minor Pentatonic and G Blues scales are used in this solo.

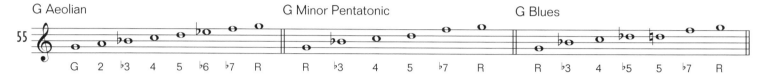

## Analysis

A G Minor Pentatonic lick in 3rd position opens this solo. The lick then travels to the 6th position and ends with a G blues scale idea on the top three strings in **bars 3–4**. The motif continues in **bars 5–6** followed by a long descending G Blues passage in **bars 7–8**.

G Minor Pentatonic—3rd Position

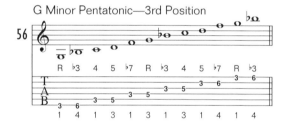 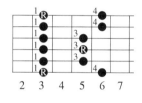

G Blues Fragment—1st–3rd strings

 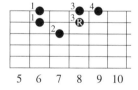

A two-note lick that uses the F and G notes is played in **bars 9–11**. This two-note pattern is repeated in three octaves with a similar rhythm.

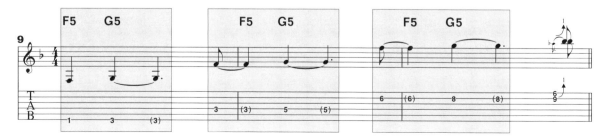

**Bars 17–22** build in intensity with ascending double stops that outline the chords. The phrase is finished with a whole-step bend to D that targets the D5 chord.

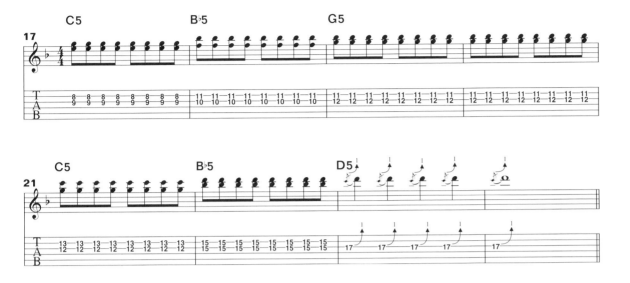

**Bars 29–32** end the solo with a G Blues scale pull-off lick using sixteenth notes on the open 3rd and 4th strings.

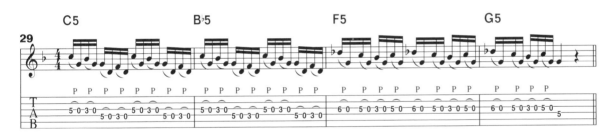

G Blues Fragment

## CHAPTER 5

### The Style of Eddie Van Halen

Eddie Van Halen began his musical training as a concert pianist. His father was an acclaimed saxophone player who gave him a foundation on which to build a career as one of the most influential guitarists in modern rock. His technical prowess, which he uses with taste and precision, has made him a legend. Combining new sounds with dazzling speed, he has made a place for himself among the ranks of guitar greats that were his primary influences. Although he cites Clapton as his favorite, Van Halen's music is also shaped by the performances of Hendrix and Blackmore. He achieves his unique style through spontaneity combined with his influences and training. Van Halen also championed the technique of *tapping*, where the right hand is used to hammer-on to a string in combination with the notes fingered by the left hand. This technique allows you to play faster, more fluid solos with less effort than picking each note.

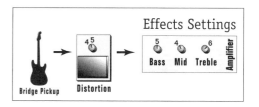

Effects Settings

Bridge Pickup → Distortion → Bass Mid Treble Amplifier

**With Solo, Track 34**
**Backing Track, Track 35**

## Caught...Two Handed!

*i* = Right-hand index finger.

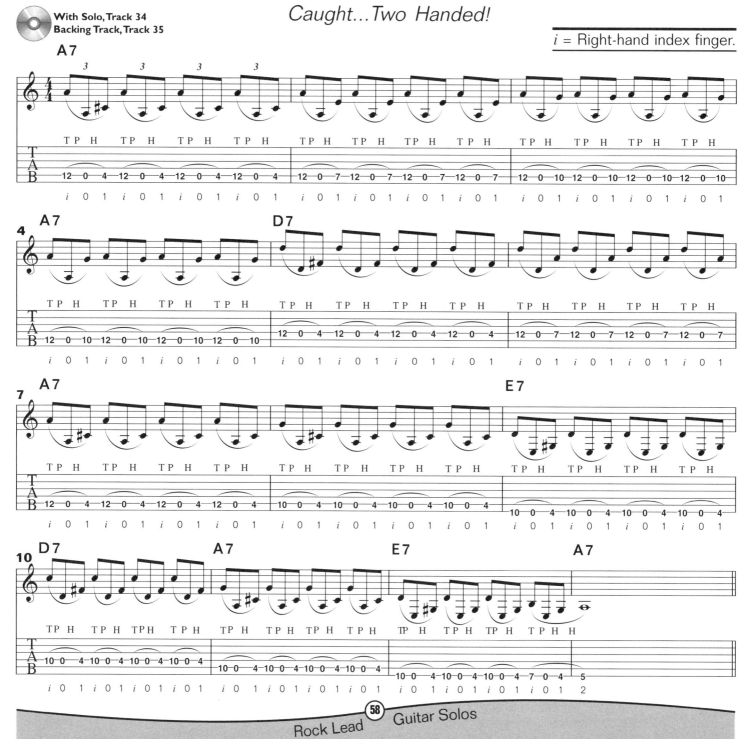

## The Chords and Scales

This two-hand tapping solo is based on a 12-bar blues in A. The chords are spelled out below.

### The Chords

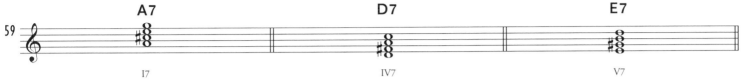

A7
I7

D7
IV7

E7
V7

### The Scales

This is not a scale-based solo. It uses single-string triplet arpeggios exclusively.

A7 Arpeggio

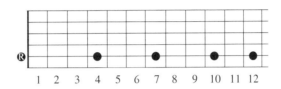

D7 Arpeggio

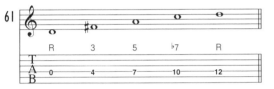

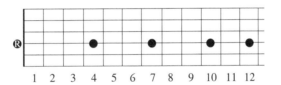

E7 Arpeggio

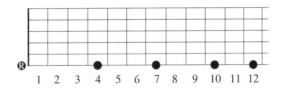

## Analysis

A7 is tapped throughout **bars 1–4**, The right hand taps the A note at the 12th fret and pulls-off to the open A. Then the left hand hammers on to other chord tones (first the 3rd, C♯; then the 5th, E; and finally the ♭7th, G).

In **bars 5–6** the idea is continued. The right hand moves to the 10th fret in **bar 6**.

The right hand first taps the 12th fret in **bar 7**, then the 10th fret in the **bar 8**.

**Bars 9–12** continue the tapped pattern, finally resting on a hammered A.

Here is another solo in the style of Eddie Van Halen. The effects settings are the same as those shown on page 58. Notice the use of *quarter tones* (intervals equal to one half of a half step) between the notes in bars 7 and 8. They represent the slow release of the bend from bar 6.

= Quarter-tone above a natural note

= Quarter-tone below a natural note

With Solo, Track 36
Backing Track, Track 37

## Eddie's Cook Book

$\frac{1}{4}$ = After striking the note, nudge the whammy bar down quickly.

$\underset{2}{\smile}$ = Use whammy bar to dive down two whole steps.

## The Chords and Scales

### The Chords

This solo is in the key of D Minor. Van Halen usually solos over a bass line only, leaving his options open for shifting the key. In this situation, the solo line, rather than the chords, determines the key. For example, while the bass guitar plays a D (root) and the guitar plays an F♯ (major 3rd), D Major is implied. If the guitar plays an F (minor 3rd), D Minor is implied.

### The Scale

This is the only scale used in this solo.

D Minor Pentatonic

## Analysis

**Bars 1–4** include D Minor Pentatonic ideas. Triplet licks using ascending and descending motifs work great in this solo. The notes used imply a minor tonality.

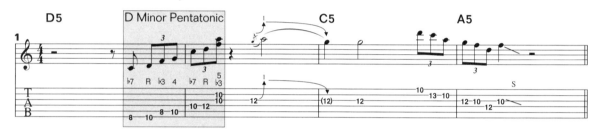

**Bars 5–8** feature a single bent note. Beginning in **bar 7** the bent note is slowly released using a *quarter-note triplet* (three quarter notes in the time of two) rhythm, giving the note a type of *choked* effect (a type of left-hand muting where the finger relaxes slightly to cut the sound short). Notice that the target note is C♯. This implies a major tonality over the A in the bass. As discussed on page 60, the bent note is released in quarter-tone increments.

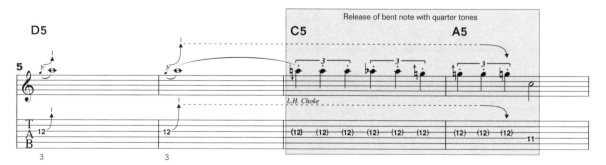

Natural harmonics appear in **bars 9–12**. The first two harmonics are Ds and the third is a G. The vibrato bar is used in **bar 12** in rhythm with the picked notes. A long vibrato-bar dive is used in **bar 13**.

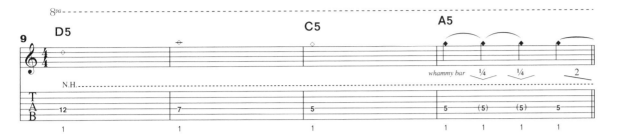

**Bars 17–20** serve up a blues triplet lick outlining the notes played in the bass.

D Major/Minor Shape

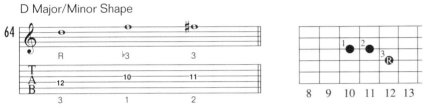

Two-hand tapping is introduced in **bars 21–24**, once again outlining the chords as they change.

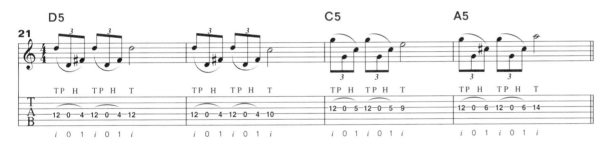

More tapped arpeggios are played in the ending section in **bars 29–33**. Notice, however, that some of the notes in these arpeggio patterns are not chord tones (shown in gray below). The G in the Dmin arpeggios adds a suspended 4th sound, and the A in the C Major arpeggios adds a CMaj6 sound. The right hand is the focus of the tapped pattern because it plays the changing tones.

Dmin Tapped Arpeggio

C Tapped Arpeggio

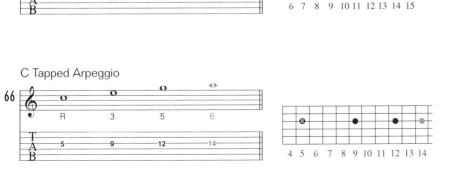

## CHAPTER 6

### The Style of Randy Rhoads

The day the legendary Randy Rhoads died was one of the saddest days in rock history. He started playing classical guitar at age 7. His biggest influence was Leslie West, although one can also hear Blackmore's influence in his playing. Rhoads combined heavy-metal histrionics with a truly musical sensibility. He will always be known for his inventiveness, grace and finesse.

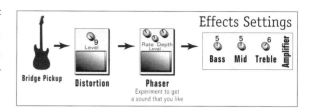

*Tapping into Oblivion*

**With Solo, Track 38**
**Backing Track, Track 39**

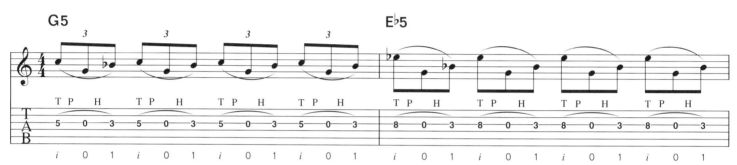

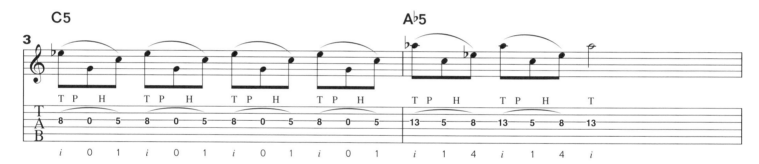

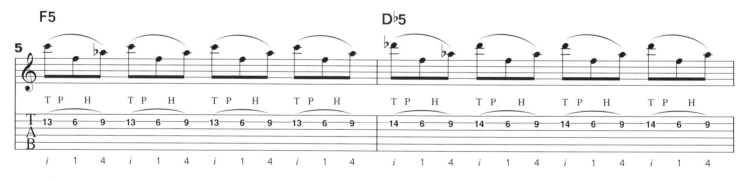

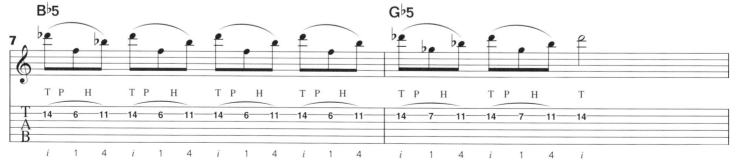

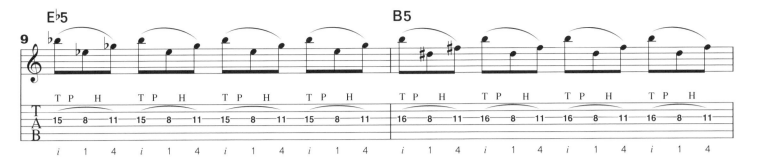

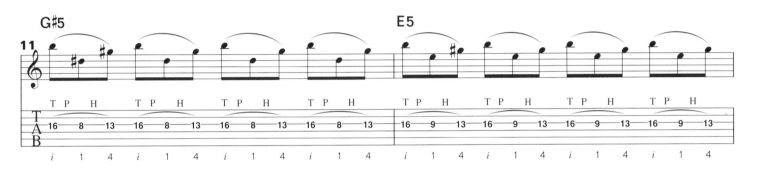

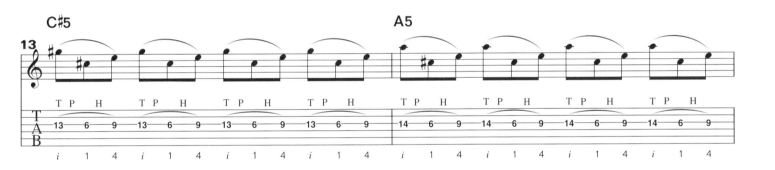

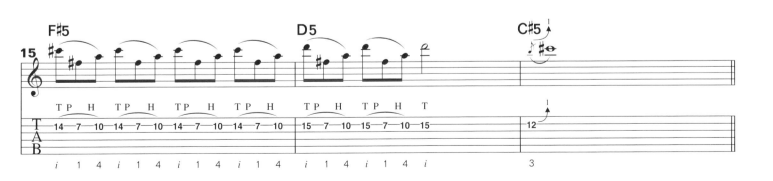

## The Chords and Scales

This Van Halen–influenced two-handed tapping extravaganza eight two-chord progressions before resting on the final C#5. Although power chords are used throughout, each two-chord vamp sets up its own key. The tonality, major or minor, is defined by the lead guitar solo.

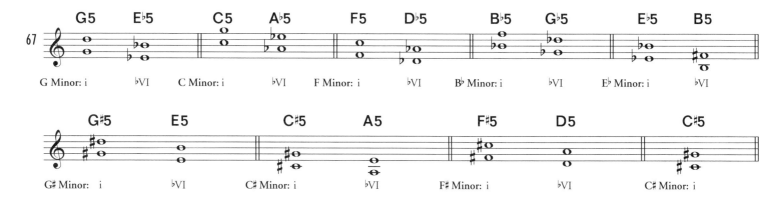

## Analysis

Triplet arpeggios are the focus of this solo. It is important to notice the same pattern is used over all 16 bars. The solo is broken down into four-bar sections. **Bars 4, 8, 12 and 16** are all related. The pattern of the notes is always a minor arpeggio followed by a major arpeggio.

**Bars 1–3** are the only measures to use an open string.

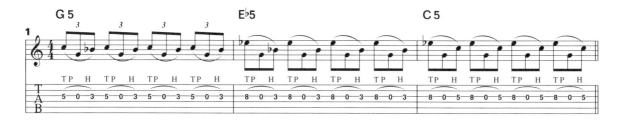

**Bars 5–6** use the right-hand tapped note to move with the chord changes. The other tones are common to both chords.

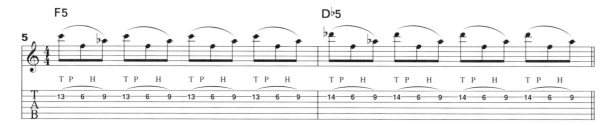

In **bars 7–8**, the 1st finger of the left hand is used to move with the chord changes. Again, the other tones are common to both chords.

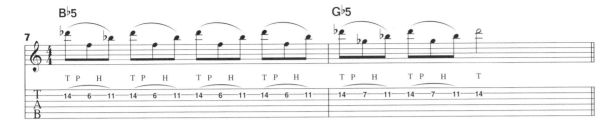

The remainder of the solo, **bars 9–16,** continue in the same manner. Practice using both the left and right hands to make chord changes while tapping. This will require that you know the notes of the chord over which you are playing. Also, knowing the notes on the string you are tapping will allow you to effortlessly change the notes as the chords change.

*As Ozzy Osbourne's guitarist, **Randy Rhoads** amazed audiences with his brilliant playing and his command of many different musical styles. He died tragically in a plane crash in 1982.*

Here is another solo in the style of Randy Rhoads.  The effects settings are the same
as those shown on page 64.

## *Aleister is About*

**With Solo, Track 40**
**Backing Track, Track 41**

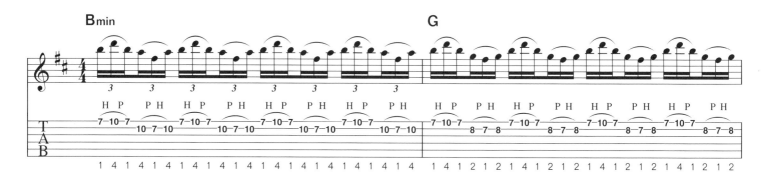

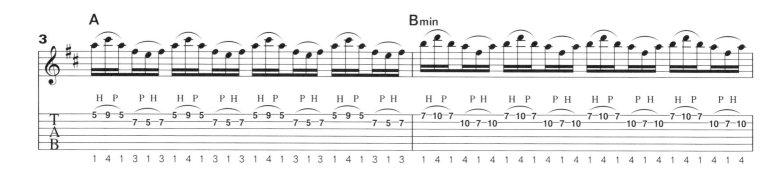

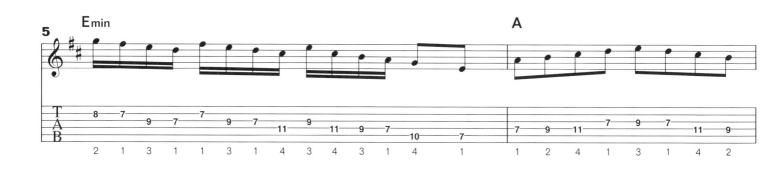

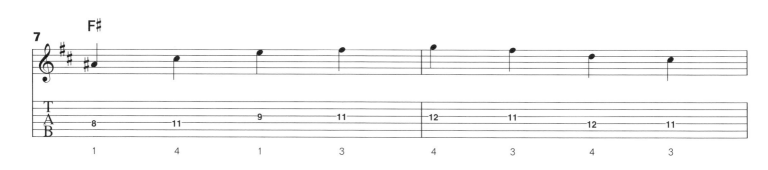

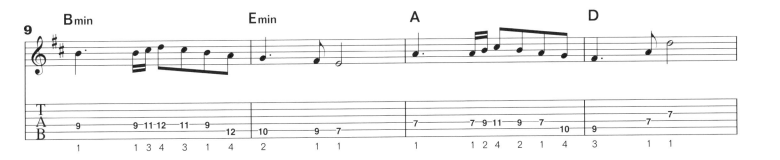

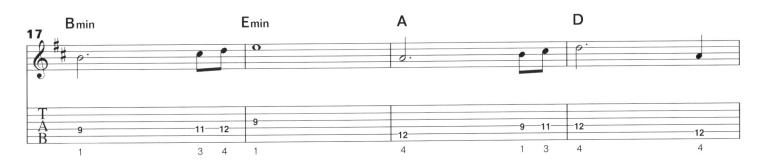

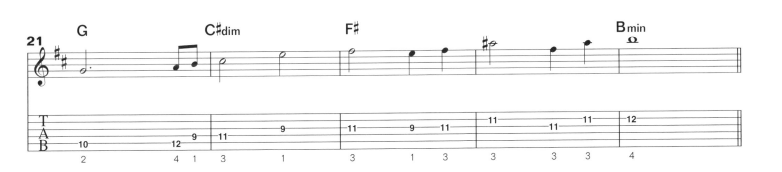

## The Chords and Scales

The key center for this dark, melodic solo is B Minor. There are two sections in this solo. The first section covers **bars 1–8**. The progression is i–♭VI–♭VII–i–iv–♭VII–V. The second section covers measures 9–24 with a i–iv–♭VII–♭III–♭VI–ii–V progression.

*The Chords*

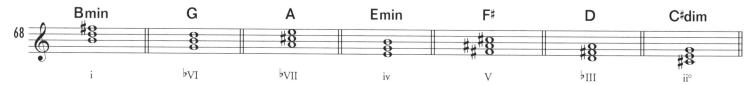

| Bmin | G | A | Emin | F# | D | C#dim |
|------|---|---|------|-----|---|-------|
| i | ♭VI | ♭VII | iv | V | ♭III | ii° |

*The Scales*

The scales used in the solo are as follows:

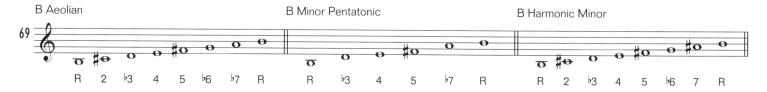

B Aeolian — R 2 ♭3 4 5 ♭6 ♭7 R

B Minor Pentatonic — R ♭3 4 5 ♭7 R

B Harmonic Minor — R 2 ♭3 4 5 ♭6 7 R

## Analysis

**Bars 1–4** fire off a blizzard of sixteenth-note triplet licks (three sixteenths in the time of two, or you can think of it as six sixteenths per beat). Each lick fits perfectly over its corresponding chord. Certain notes are adjusted to fit the particular chord being played without noticeably changing the lick. For example, the second half of the Bmin sextuplet in **bar 1** is subtly changed when the chord changes to G in **bar 2**.

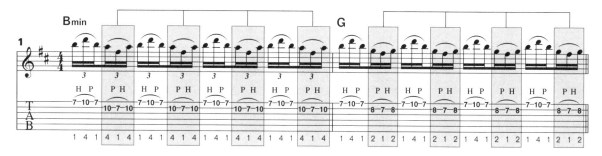

A cool sequenced motif derived from the B Aeolian scale is used in **bars 5–6.**

B Aeolian—7th Position

The ending of the first section comes in **bars 7–8** over the F# chord. An F#7 arpeggio and B Harmonic Minor scale fragments are used effectively.

F#7 Arpeggio

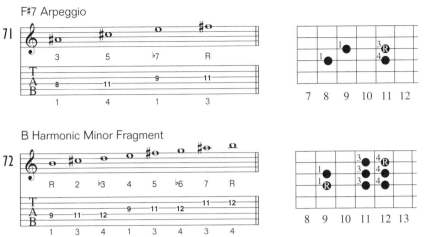

B Harmonic Minor Fragment

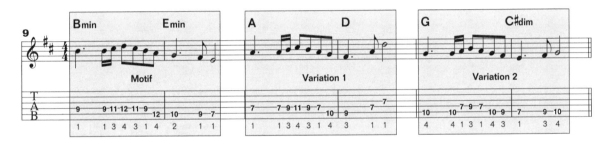

In **bars 9–10** a new section begins with a new motif from the B Aeolian scale (page 70). The motif is repeated with a slight variation in **bars 11–14**.

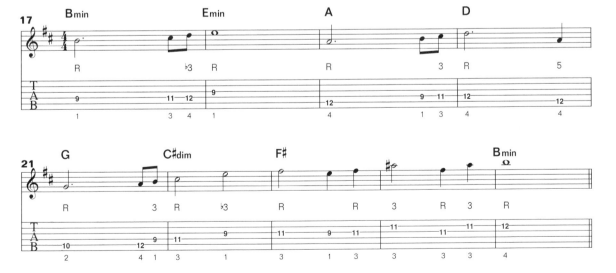

The ending, **bars 17–24**, are made of a long, ascending, singable melody that targets chord roots as the harmony changes.

NWOBHM, or New Wave of British Heavy Metal, came on the scene in the late 1970s and early 1980s. Bands including Judas Priest, Iron Maiden and Def Leppard came from "across the pond" with a very new-sounding hard rock. With their precision, speed and use of other scales in addition to the long-favored minor pentatonic scale, the NWOBHM guitarists created a whole new approach to soloing.

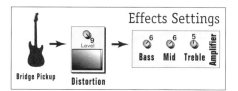

## From Across the Pond

**With Solo, Track 42**
**Backing Track, Track 43**

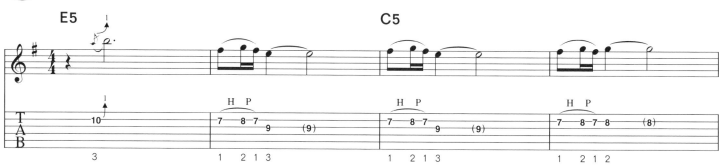

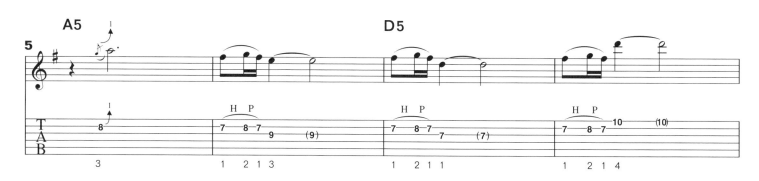

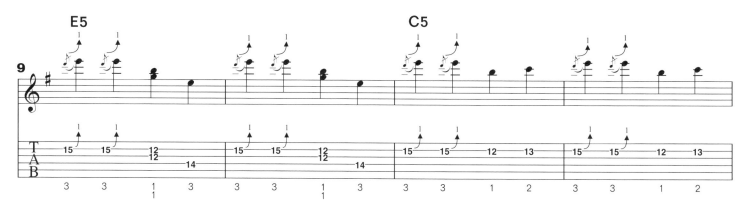

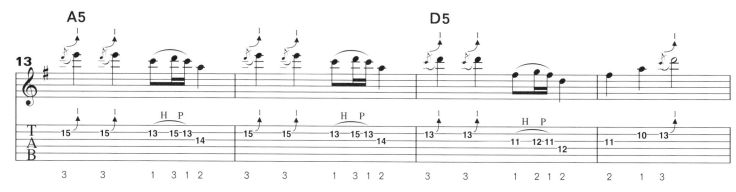

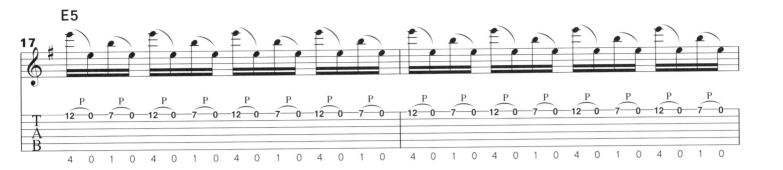

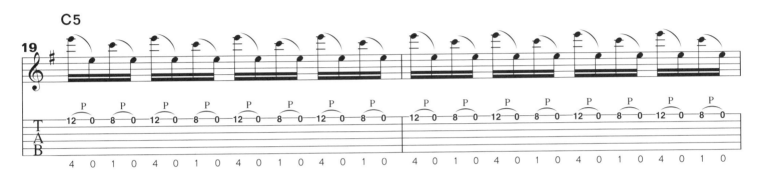

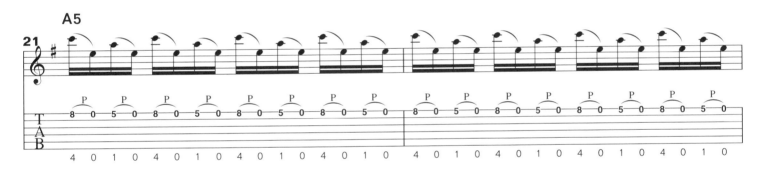

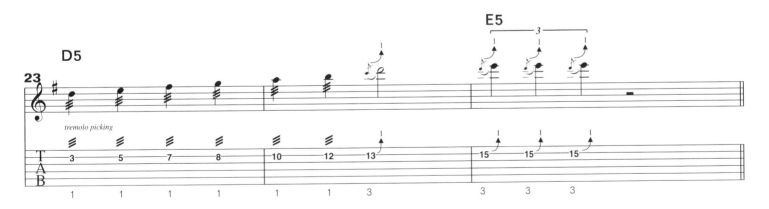

## The Chords and Scales

This heavy-metal rocker is in the key of E Minor. The progression is i–VI–iv–♭VII and uses power chords. The chords are spelled out below.

*The Chords*

*The Scales*

The scales used in this solo are:

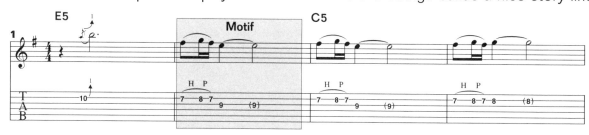

## Analysis

After the initial bend in **bar 1**, a melodic motif is introduced in **bar 2** and carries through **bars 3–8**. The idea is built from the E Aeolian scale in the 7th position. This simple motif played on the 2nd and 3rd strings builds a nice story line.

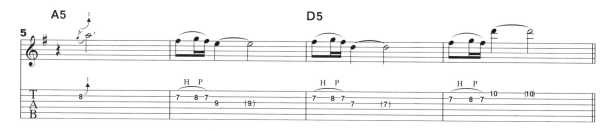

E Aeolian—7th Position Fragment

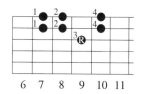

**Bars 9–16** mix the minor pentatonic scale and Aeolian mode to create the middle section of the solo.

E Aeolian—12th Position Fragment

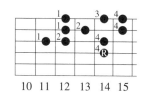

Notice that each motif is primarily composed of consists chord tones.

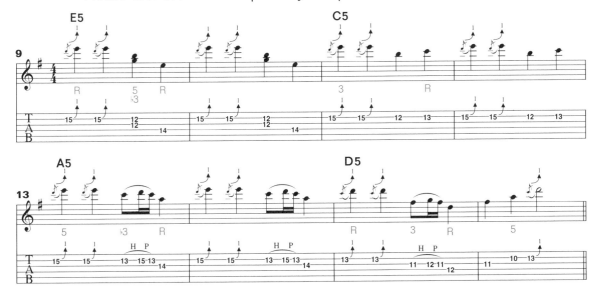

A sixteenth-note single-string *pedal-tone* lick is played repeatedly in **bars 17–22**. A pedal tone is a note that remains the same as the harmony changes; in this case, E. The open E string is used along with pull-offs from notes from the E Aeolian mode relating to each chord. **Bars 18 and 19** show how this works.

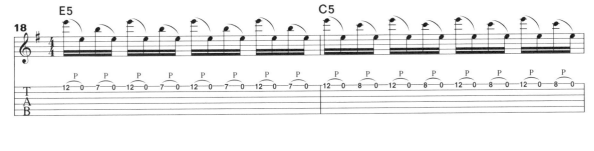

### E Aeolian—1st String

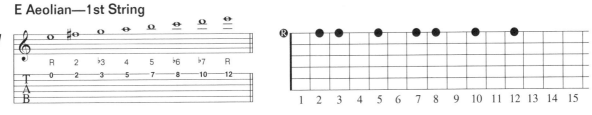

A *tremolo-picked* ascending passage is applied over the D5 chord in **bars 23–24**, coming to rest on an E. Tremolo picking is the rapid repetition of a single note by alternating downstrokes and upstrokes. This is a great explosive way of ending a solo in this style.

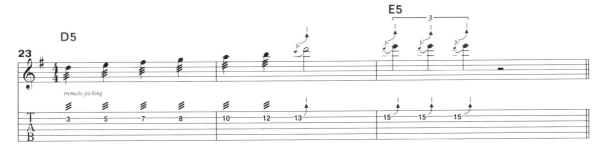

The following solo is based on the solo from pages 72–73. Many NWOBHM bands used the twin-guitar attack with harmonized guitar solos. Here is a harmonized version of *From Across the Pond.*

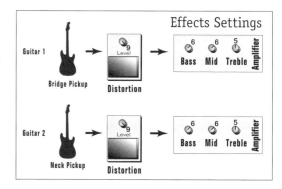

**With Solo, Track 44**
**Backing Track, Track 45**

## And Then There Were Two
*(From Across the Pond, Harmonized)*

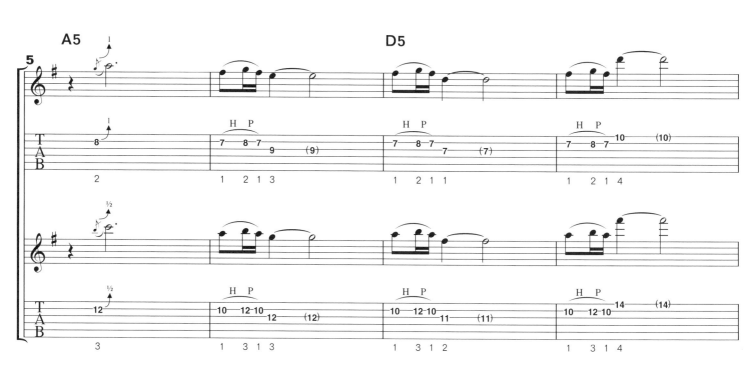

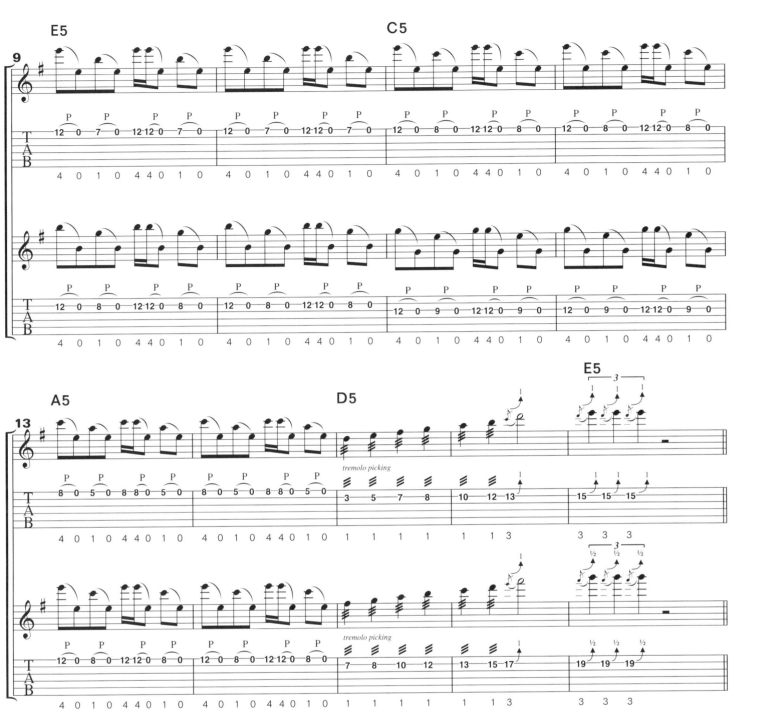

## The Chords and Scales

### The Chords
See example 70 on page 74. This is the same chord progression.

### The Scales
Both guitars use the same scales. The second guitar harmonizes in 3rds, 4ths or 5ths above the first guitar.

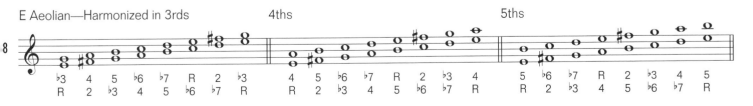

## Analysis

In **bars 1–8**, Guitar 2 plays in 3rds above Guitar 1. Listen to the CD and notice that Guitar 2 perfectly mirrors Guitar 1 in rhythm and dynamics.

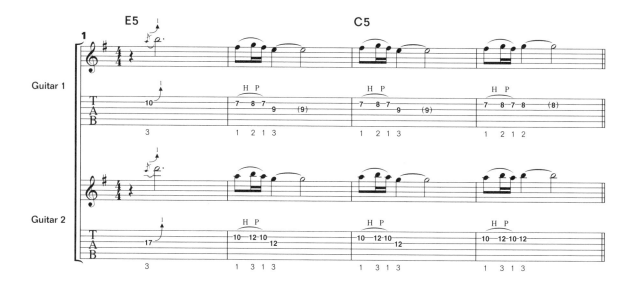

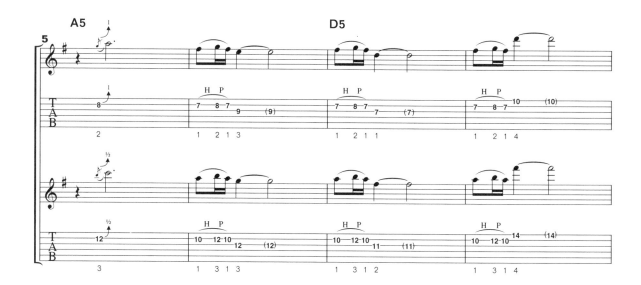

In **bars 9–12**, the harmony moves below the melody. The open 2nd string of Guitar 2 is used to harmonize with the open 1st string of Guitar 1. When both guitars play these open strings, a perfect 4th is produced. The same harmonic interval is produced when both guitars play notes at the 12th fret. The harmony of a 3rd is produced when Guitar 1 plays the B and Guitar 2 plays the G. **Bars 11–12** use more harmonies in 3rds.

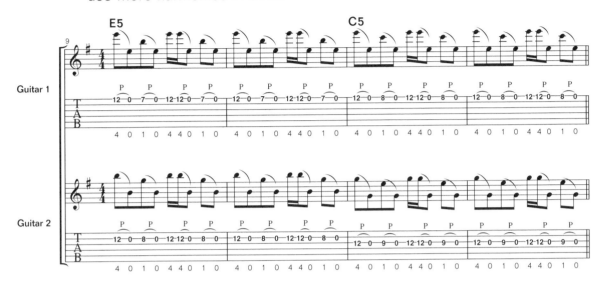

Learning the E Aeolian mode on each of the first three strings will help.

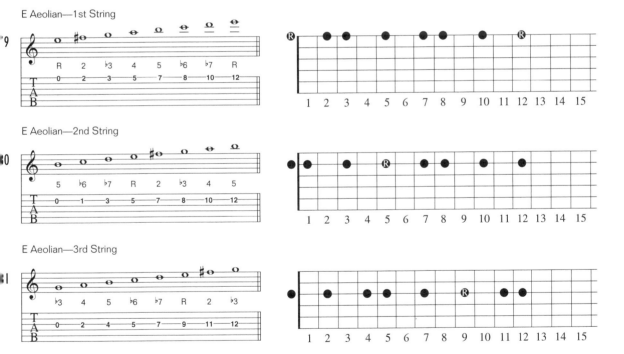

Guitar 2 harmonizes a 3rd above Guitar 1 for the tremolo-picked passage in **bars 15–16**.

## The Style of Kirk Hammett

Kirk Hammett's furious and aggressive soloing style is influenced by KISS, Jimi Hendrix and Michael Schenker of U.F.O. He is best known as the lead guitarist of the heavy metal band Metallica, and has a style that serves up blues licks without sounding like blues at all. He has a knack for taking minor pentatonic scales and turning them into a work of art.

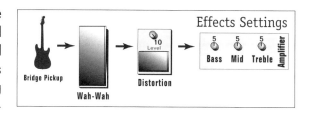

 **With Solo, Track 46**
**Backing Track, Track 47**

## Horror Movie Metal

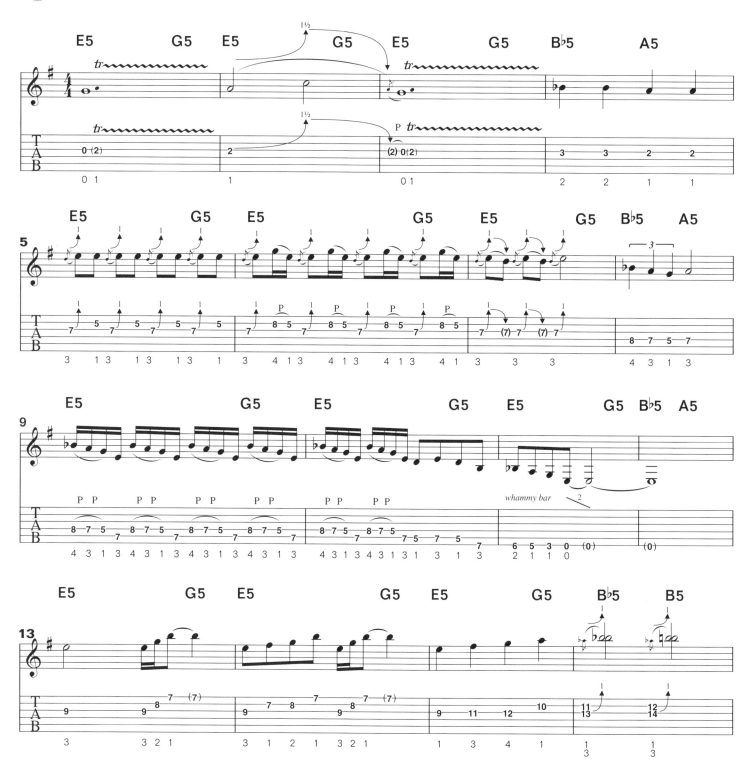

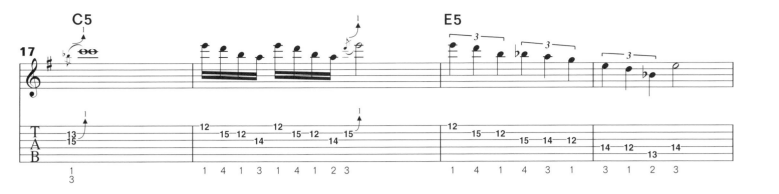

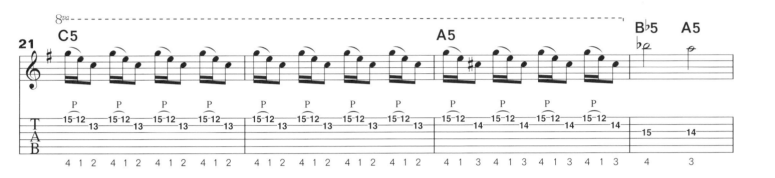

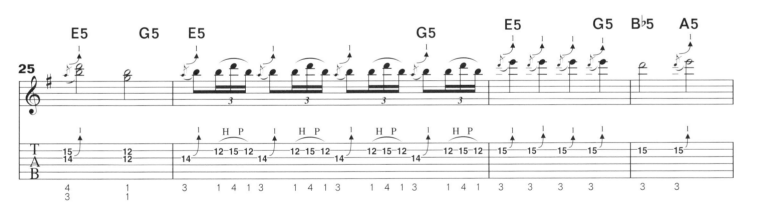

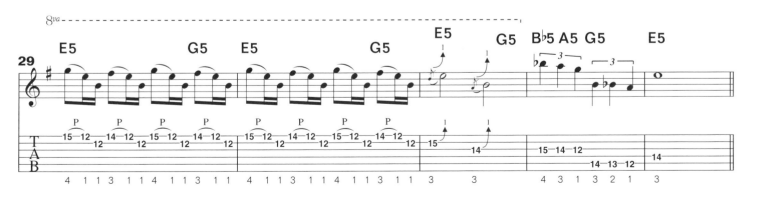

## The Chords and Scales

### The Chords

This thrash metal solo is in E Minor. The progression is split between two sections: The main progression is i–III–i–III–i–III–♭V–iv; the progression of the second section is VI–i–VI–iv. All of the chords are power chords.

Think of the B♭5 chord as a *passing chord* (a chord outside of the key that is used to move smoothly between chords within the key).

### The Scales

The following scales are used:

## Analysis

**Bars 1–4** open with a trill using the open 3rd string followed by a long bend and release which is reminicent of the style of Jimi Hendrix. **Bar 4** hits the respective roots of the B♭5 and A5 chord.

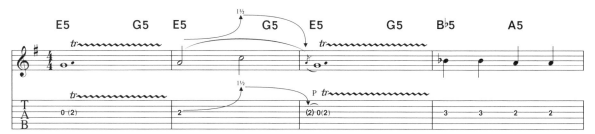

Cool blues-scale licks keep the energy up through **bars 5–6**. **Bar 7** finishes off the lick using bend and release tactics. **Bar 8** uses a quarter-note triplet phrase, emphasizing the chord roots once again.

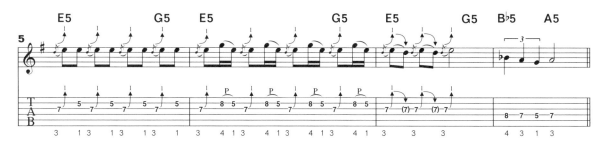

**Bar 9** blasts into a series of sixteenth-note pull-offs colored by the ♭5 of the blues scale. This idea connects through to **bar 12** where the blues scale descends to the open 6th string. Once the open E string is struck, the vibrato bar is pushed all the way down to create a low crashing effect.

A new idea is established using an E Minor arpeggio in 7th position in **bars 13–14**.

Emin Arpeggio

**Bar 16** cleverly follows the chords with a series of unison bends.

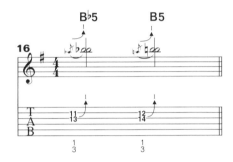

An arpeggio idea is built over the chords in **bars 21–23**. A C Major arpeggio is used over the C5 chord. An A7 arpeggio is used over the A5.

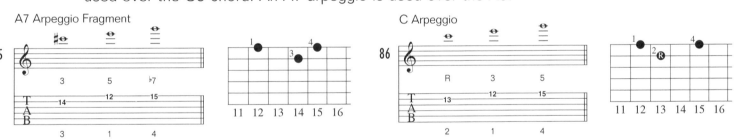

A7 Arpeggio Fragment

C Arpeggio

The ending, **bars 25–33**, burn on E Blues licks, bringing the solo to its close. Many of the licks are repeated two or four times.

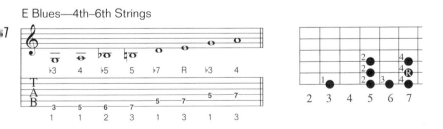

E Blues—4th–6th Strings

Neoclassical solos are a melding of classical-style melodies and modern rock sounds performed at blinding speed. This combination brings a touch of class to the otherwise harsh sound of the heavy metal riff. Yngwie Malmsteen and Vinnie Moore are two well-known shredders who like to apply the grace of classical pieces to their guitar styles. Many believe neoclassical soloing was pioneered by the virtuosity of Randy Rhoads.

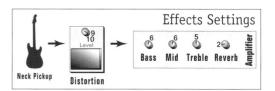

**With Solo, Track 48**
**Backing Track, Track 49**

*Bach Lives*

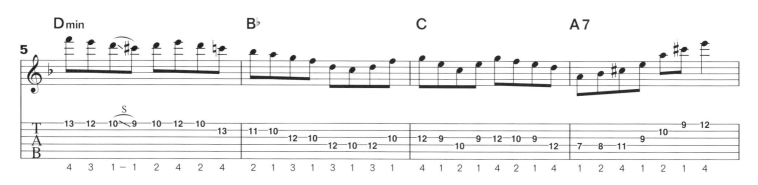

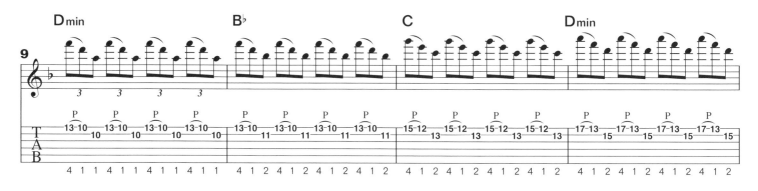

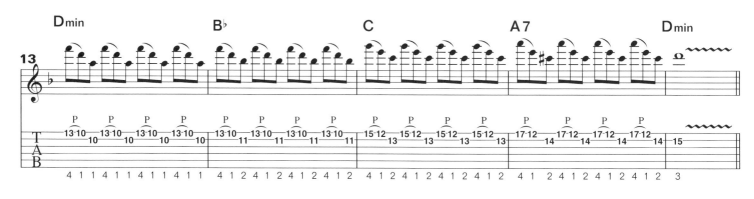

## The Chords and Scales

This classical influenced progression is in the key of D Minor. The progression is
i–VI–♭VII–i–VI–♭VII–V. The chords are spelled out below.

### The Chords

### The Scales

The scales used are as follows:

## Analysis

**Bar 1** opens with a harmonic minor idea, then immediately ascends using D Aeolian mode. **Bars 2–4** continue ascending, targeting chord tones over each chord. This phrase ends in **bar 4** with a bent A over the Dmin chord.

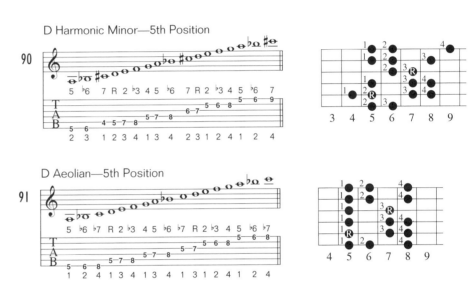

The next four **bars (5–8)** respond to the first four by keeping the same motif—this time descending through the D Aeolian scale. In **bar 8** the D Harmonic Minor scale is used to create a lick over the A7 chord, creating a sound reminiscent of J.S. Bach.

A series of arpeggios finish out the solo in the **last 8 bars**. Each arpeggio corresponds with the chord underneath.

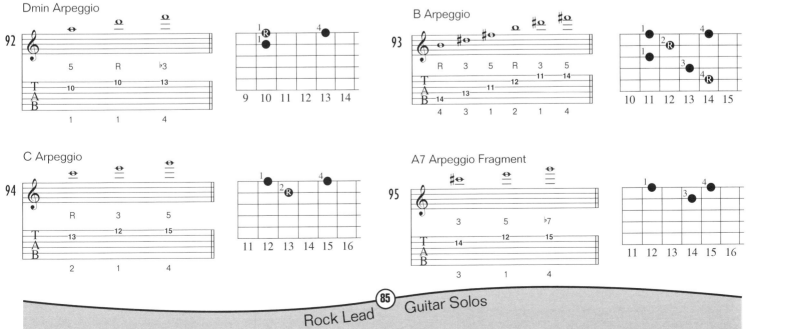

## CHAPTER 7

### The Style of Steve Vai

Considered one of rock's more original guitarists, Steve Vai has taken rock soloing to the extreme. Vai does not take his music lightly and has been known to use unconventional means to reach his goals. His music has great feeling and often evokes more emotions than mainstream rock. His melodies flow effortlessly while displaying an array of shifting sounds and textures. Vai's Frank Zappa influences meld nicely with his breathtaking virtuosity.

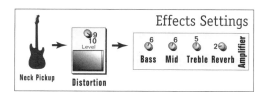

**With Solo, Track 50**
**Backing Track, Track 51**

## *Ask the Ouija Board*

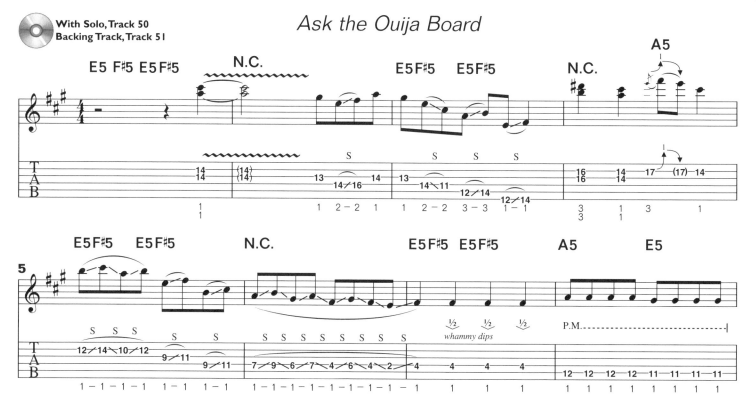

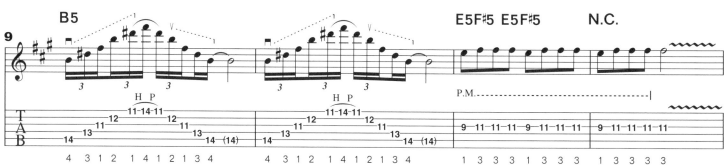

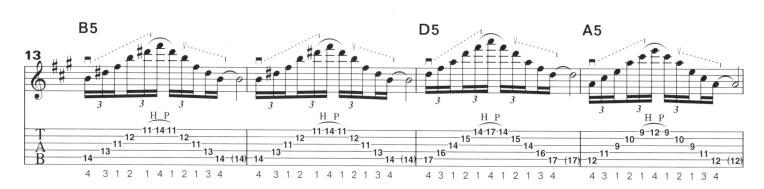

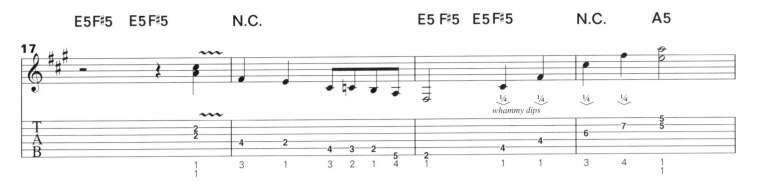

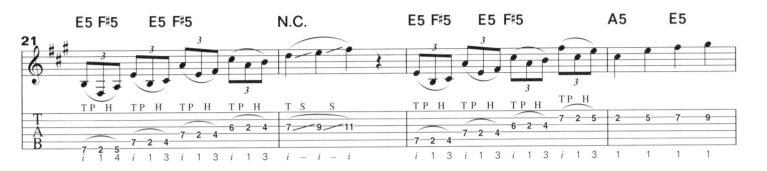

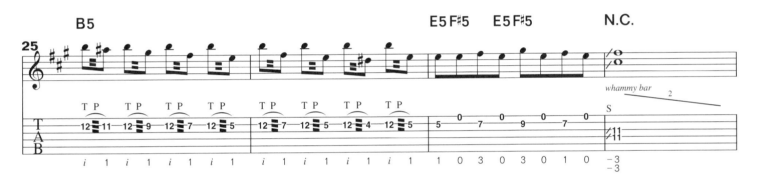

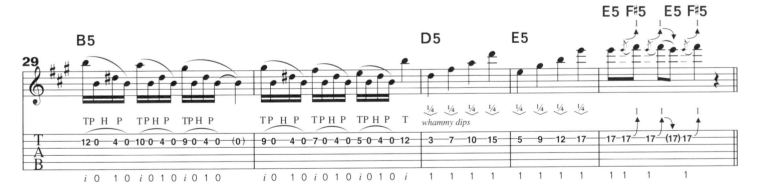

$\frac{1}{4}$ = After striking the note, nudge the whammy bar down quickly.

$\underset{\displaystyle 2}{\diagdown}$ = Use whammy bar to dive down two whole steps.

and = Tremolo. Rapid alteration between two notes.

## The Chords and Scales

### The Chords

This solo is in the key of F♯ Minor. The progression is *riff*-based (a riff is a short repeated accompaniment pattern) and uses power chords with a slight funk groove. The chords are spelled out below.

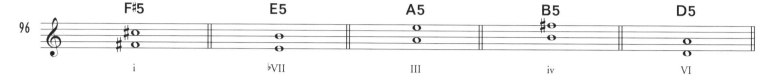

### The Scales

The scales used in the solo are as follows.

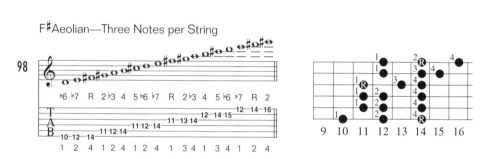

## Analysis

This solo begins on the fourth beat of **bar 1** with a double stop followed by a sliding idea in **bar 2** from the F♯ Aeolian mode/Pentatonic scale (all of the notes in the minor pentatonic scale are also in the Aeolian mode). This idea stretches through **bar 3**. Double stops and a bend-and-release lick follow over the A5 chord in **bar 4**.

A descending scale lick using slides over **bars 5–6** flows right into the root (F♯) in **bar 7**, where the vibrato bar dips are used as the notes are picked. A steady, palm-muted eighth-note transition appears in **bar 8**.

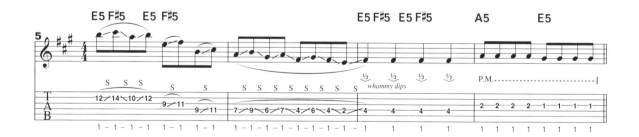

B Major arpeggios using *sweep picking* fly over the B5 chord in **bars 9–10** (shown top of next page). Sweep picking is playing a passage across several strings with a successive movement of the pick in either a downward or upward direction.

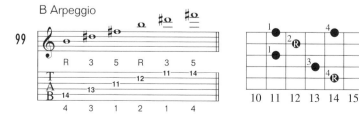

Palm-muted notes from the F♯ Minor Pentatonic scale fill in **bars 11–12**.

The sweep-picked major arpeggios in **bars 13–16** outline each chord starting with B and moving to D and A in **bars 15–16**—plus it just sounds awesome!

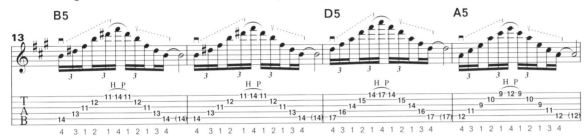

**Bars 21–24** use a two-hand tapped minor pentatonic lick.

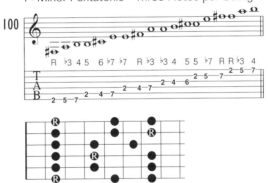

F♯ Minor Pentatonic—Three Notes per String

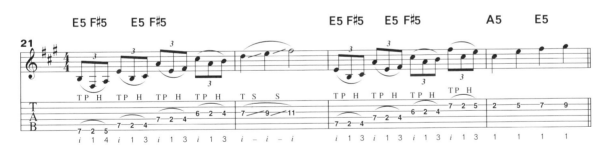

**Bars 29–32** use more two-hand tapping, lending a B Major flavor to the B5 chord. An ascending F♯ Aeolian scale passage on the 2nd string follows. Note the whammy-bar dips on each note.

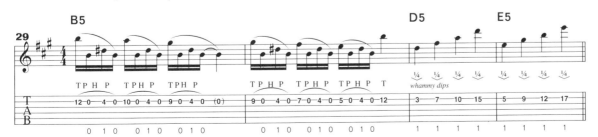

## The Future—Progressive

Only time will tell what the future holds for the rock guitar solo. From the playing of Jimi Hendrix to Eddie Van Halen to Steve Vai, the rock guitar solo has taken many twists and turns and will forever be evolving. Progressive rock, or "prog-rock," is a style that offers many opportunities for new ways of soloing. Players like John Petrucci (Dream Theater, Liquid Tension Experiment) push the envelope by using odd time and frequent key changes. This solo alternates between $\frac{4}{4}$ and $\frac{7}{8}$.

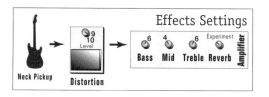

Effects Settings

**With Solo, Track 52**
**Backing Track, Track 53**

## Time and Space

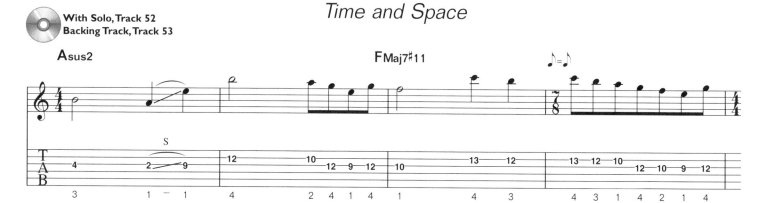

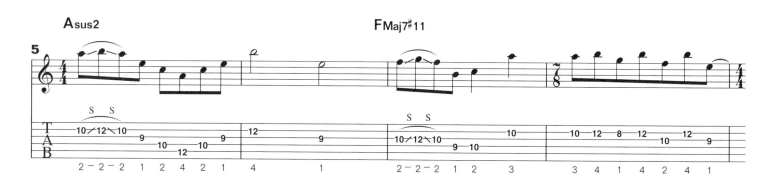

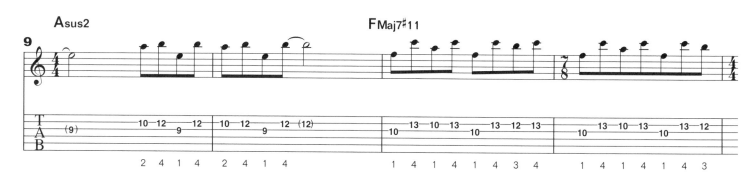

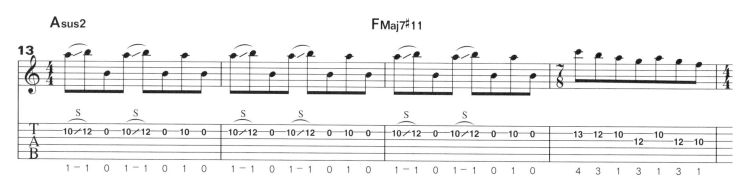

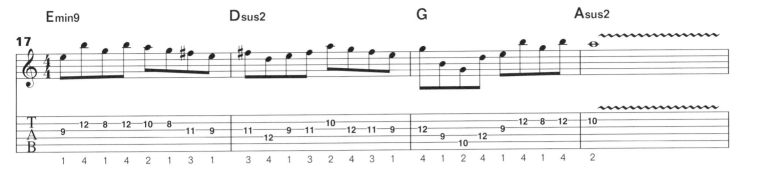

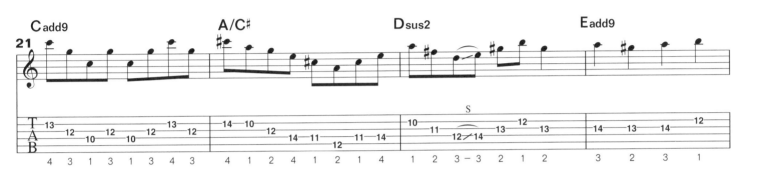

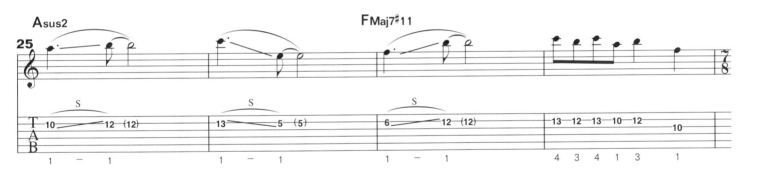

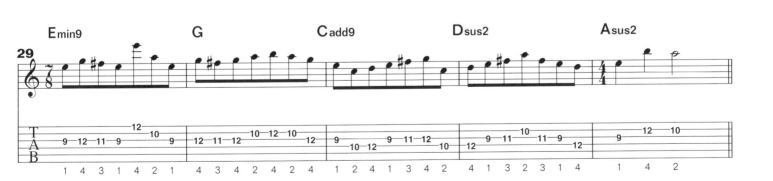

## The Chords and Scales

This spacey prog-rock solo is in the key of A Minor, however in this style of soloing it is common to think of each chord as its own key center.

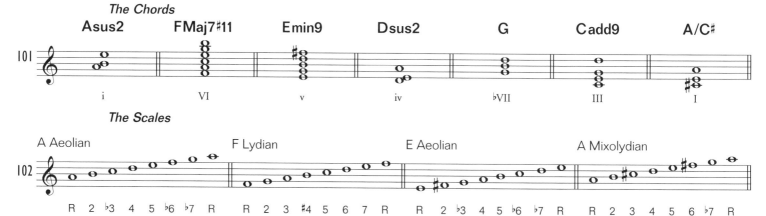

*The Chords*

| Asus2 | FMaj7#11 | Emin9 | Dsus2 | G | Cadd9 | A/C# |
|-------|----------|-------|-------|---|-------|------|
| i | VI | v | iv | ♭VII | III | I |

*The Scales*

A Aeolian   F Lydian   E Aeolian   A Mixolydian

R 2 ♭3 4 5 ♭6 ♭7 R    R 2 3 #4 5 6 7 R    R 2 ♭3 4 5 ♭6 ♭7 R    R 2 3 4 5 6 ♭7 R

## Analysis

This solo uses $\frac{7}{8}$ time, which is classified as *odd time* (a time signature where the number of beats per measure is greater than four and not divisible by two, such as $\frac{5}{4}$, $\frac{7}{8}$ and $\frac{11}{8}$). You can think of $\frac{7}{8}$ time as $\frac{4}{4}$ with one eighth note subtracted. Instead of 1–&–2–&–3–&–4, just count even eighth notes (1–2–3–4–5–6–7). The tempo of the eighth note remains constant when the time signatures change. This may take a while to get used to. Listen to the CD and practice counting while reading along with the solo on pages 90–91.

The solo opens with chord tones and a slide on the 3rd string. The F Lydian scale is used over the FMaj7#11 chord in **bars 3–4**.

F Lydian—Three Notes per String

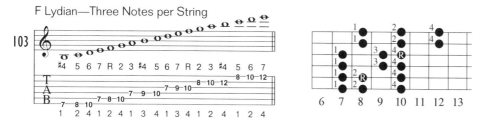

An A Minor add9 arpeggio is used in **bars 5–6**. A pivoting lick (a lick that revolves around a specific pitch, in this case B, which is the #11 of the chord) is used during the $\frac{7}{8}$ time in **bar 8**.

Amin add9 Arpeggio

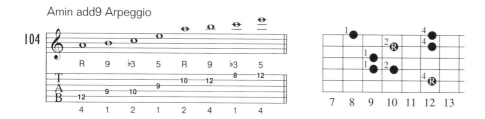

A disorienting slide lick that uses the open 2nd string appears in **bars 13–15**.

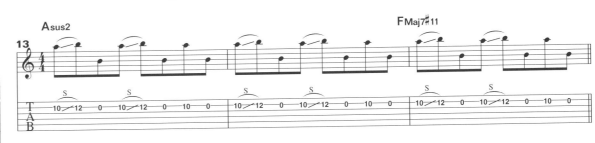

**Bars 17–24** are constructed primarily of arpeggios outlining each chord.

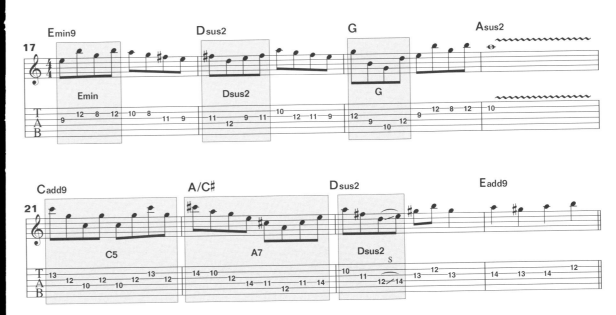

**Bars 29–32** are all in $\frac{7}{8}$ time. The constant stream of eighth-note arpeggios works wonderfully over the chords and is intensified by the rhythm guitar.

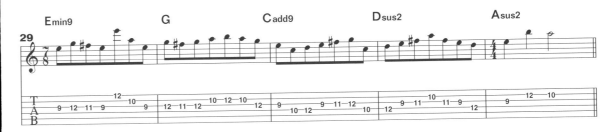

**Congratulations for completing *Rock Lead Guitar Solos*!** You have been exposed to some of the most important styles and techniques in rock improvisation. Never stop experimenting and learning about different styles of music. Whether it's jazz, classical or from some far-off, exotic place, this will make you a better rock player. Keep practicing and have fun!

Here is a glossary of some of the most frequently used and important rock guitar techniques. It is by no means complete, but will help with most situations that arise in this book.

### Bend

Strike the note and bend it up one whole step (the sound of the note two frets above the starting pitch). Notice the use of a *grace note* (a small, quick, decorative note). Bend notation also includes a *slur* ⌐. With a slur, only the first note is plucked.

### Bend and Release

Bend the first note as indicated. Then, release it back to the original note in the rhythm shown. Only the first note is plucked.

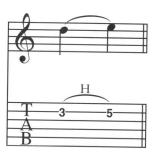

### Hammer-on

Hammer-ons are indicated with a slur. Strike the first note then slam a left-hand finger down so that the second (higher) note sounds without being plucked.

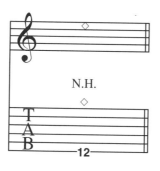

### Natural Harmonic

Strike the string while the left-hand finger lightly touches directly over the indicated fret.

### Palm Muting

Lightly rest the edge of the right hand on the strings next to the bridge to produce a slightly muted sound.

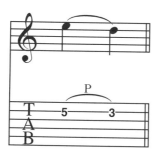

### Pull-off

Pull-offs are indicated with a slur. Put both fingers on the notes to be played. Strike the first note, then pull that finger down (towards the floor) so that the second note sounds without being plucked.

### Slide
Strike the first note, then slide the finger along the string to the second note. Do not strike the second note.

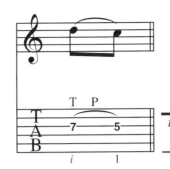
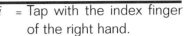

### Tapping
Sound the notes by hammering-on with a right-hand finger.

*i* = Tap with the index finger of the right hand.

### Tremolo Picking
Repeat the note rapidly by alternating downstrokes and upstrokes.

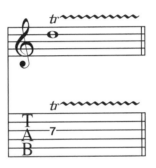

### Trill
Pick the first note and then perform a series of rapid hammer-ons and pull-offs to the note a diatonic 2nd above the first note for the duration of the note value indicated.

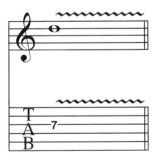

### Vibrato
Rapidly bend and release the note with the left hand or vibrato bar to create an expressive, vocal, vibrating sound.

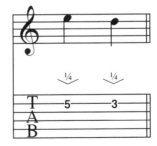

### Whammy Dip
Press the whammy bar down slightly to drop the pitch of the indicated note.

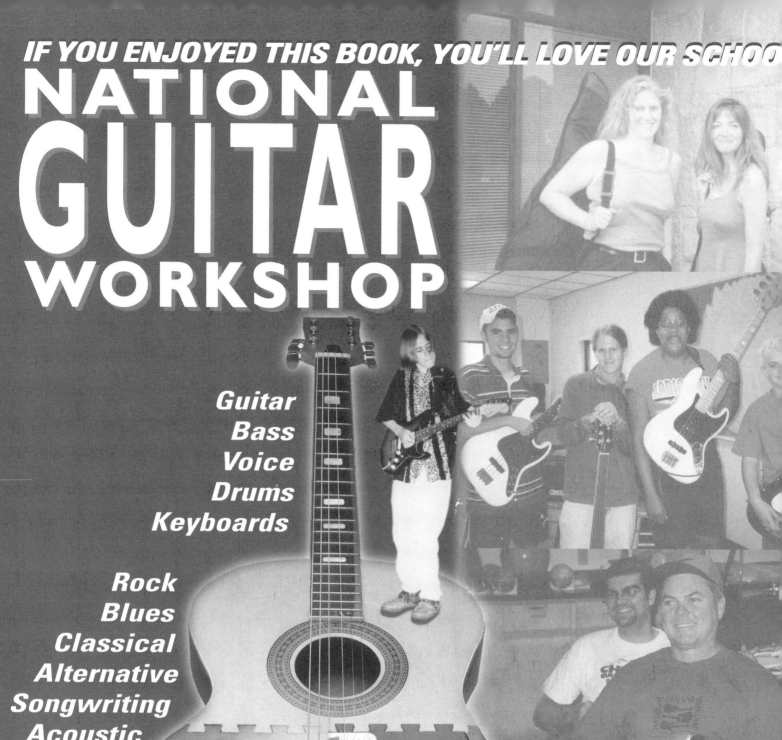